Heroes of Argenteuil Duty, Service and Sacrifice

The stories of Argenteuil men in conflicts of the 20th and 21st Centuries

Danny Bouchard M.B., P.L.C.G.S.

Printed and published in 2014

ISBN 978-0-9936096-0-2

Danny Bouchard
Lachute, Québec
info@canadiangenealogyandresearch.ca

http://canadiangenealogyandresearch.ca/

Photos cover page: Lachute cenotaph (author) with the Bretteville-Sur-Laize Canadian War Cemetery in watermark, courtesy of the Commonwealth War Graves Commission.

Acknowledgment

This book would not have been possible without the assistance and cooperation of certain people and organizations. I wish to thank Mr. Roger Duplantie, General Manager, La Compagnie d'Edition André Paquette Inc., for granting me permission to use any material from the newspaper The Watchman and to the staff of the newspaper L'Argenteuil - Tribune Express in Lachute, for allowing me access to their office in order to view microfilms.

Am also indebted to family members of our Fallen, who allowed the use of their photographs in this work.

Lastly, I want to thank my wife for her support, her assistance and for putting up with me and my laptop computer!

To our Soldiers, Sailors and Airmen!!

Foreword

This book is dedicated to the men of Argenteuil County who braved their fears and enlisted in the Armies, Air Forces and Navies of Canada and Britain in times of War and made the ultimate sacrifice. Canada found herself involved in wars in which the world would change forever. From the trenches of World War One to battling insurgents in Afghanistan and the numerous United Nations peacekeeping missions, Canadians have always been in the forefront of conflict, and volunteers from Argenteuil have always been numerous. During 1914-1919, volunteers from the County certainly didn't imagine the horrors waiting for them in the Fields of Flanders. From the massive use of artillery, machineguns and poison gas, our soldiers braved these weapons daily. Imagine... the bravery of every soldier, ordered to leave the relative safety of their trenches to cross No Man's Land in order to charge the enemy trench under murderous fire!! How many acts of bravery were performed and never documented for lack of eyewitnesses??

The biographies are listed alphabetically by surname for ease of research and were written using primary archival textual records and well researched secondary sources when the primary sources were not available. Soldiers service files, unit's war diaries, squadron's operational record books and other records from Archival repositories in Canada, Great-Britain, the United States and even from South Africa, were consulted, copied, studied and carefully analyzed to insure accurate biographical information. Every effort was made not to omit any soldiers. If some are missing, please feel free to contact the author.

Numerous Argenteuil men also enlisted in the Royal Canadian Air Force as bomber crews. These men were sent on raids over Germany, Italy and wherever else they were called on, risking their lives on long flights, often never to be seen again.

Criterias for inclusion - Locations

In order to qualify for inclusion in this publication, the deceased servicemen had to have a connection to Argenteuil County and/or be mentioned on the War Memorial cenotaph and monuments of Lachute, Brownsburg, St-André and Arundel. This connection includes but is not limited to having been born and raised in Argenteuil, parents residing in Argenteuil or having themselves lived in Argenteuil for some time.

The following locations were/are all part of Argenteuil County:

- Arundel
- Avoca
- Brownsburg
- Calumet
- Carillon
- Chatham
- Dalesville
- Dunany
- Edina
- Gore
- Grenville
- Harrington
- Huberdeau
- Lac-Saint-Denis
- Lac-des-Seize-Îles
- Lachute
- Lakefield
- Lakeview

- Laurel
- Lost-River
- Mille-Isles
- Montfort
- Morin-Heights
- Ogdensburg
- Pointe-au-Chêne
- Saint-Adolphe-d'Howard
- Saint-Andrews
- Saint-André-Est
- Saint-André-d'Argenteuil
- Saint-Michel-de-Wentworth
- Stonefield
- Thomas' Gore
- Weir
- Wentworth
- All other villages and hamlets of the old Argenteuil County.

Abbreviations

B.G.S. = Bombing and Gunnery School
Bn = Battalion
C.C.S. = Casualty Clearing Station
C.C.S. = Canadian Chaplain Services
C.C.A.C. = Canadian Casualty Assembly Centre
C.E.F. = Canadian Expeditionary Force
C.F.A. = Canadian Field Artillery
C.F.C. = Canadian Forestry Corps
C.E.R.U. = Canadian Engineers Reinforcement Unit
C.I.R.U. = Canadian Infantry Reinforcement Unit
C.M.R. = Canadian Mounted Rifles
C.Q.M.S. = Company Quarter Master Sergeant
C.R.T. = Canadian Railway Troops
E.F.T.S. = Elementary Flying Training School
F.P. No.1 = Field punishment number 1
G.G.F.G. = Governor General's Foot Guards
H.M.H.S. = His Majesty's Hospital Ship
H.M.S. = His Majesty's Ship
H.M.T. = His Majesty's Troopship

I.T.S. = Initial Training School
K.T.S. = Composite Training School (RCAF)
MiD = Mentioned in Despatches
N.C.O. = Non Commissioned Officer
P.O.W. = Prisoner of War
P.P.C.L.I. = Princess Patricia's Canadian Light Infantry
R.A.F. = Royal Air Force
R.C.A.F. = Royal Canadian Air Force
R.F.C. = Royal Flying Corps
R.H.R. = The Black Watch (Royal Highland Regiment) of Canada
R.I.R. = Royal Irish Rifles
R.N. = Royal Navy
R.R. of C. = Royal Rifles of Canada
S.F.T.S. = Service Flying Training School
S.S.F. = Special Service Force

Definitions

Harvest Leave: A period of leave granted to soldiers who were working on farms immediately before they joined for duty. This was for a six week period and was without pay. This leave was to work on a specified farm but not necessarily on that farm on which the soldier was previously working. This was announced by the Militia Department on August 9th, 1918.

Batman: A soldier assigned to an officer as a servant.

Field punishment No.1: Where an offender is sentenced to field punishment No. 1, he may, during the continuance of his sentence, unless the court martial or the commanding officer otherwise directs, be punished as follows:
(a) He may be kept in irons, i.e., in fetters or handcuffs, or both fetters and handcuffs; and may be secured so as to prevent his escape.

(b) When in irons he may be attached for a period or periods not exceeding two hours in any one day to a fixed object, but he must not be so attached during more than three out of any four consecutive days, nor during more than twenty-one days in all.
(c) Straps or ropes may be used for the purpose of these rules in lieu of irons.
(d) He may be subjected to the like labour, employment, and restraint, and dealt with in like manner as if he were under a sentence of imprisonment with hard labour.[1]

[1] Manual of Military Law, 5th Edition, 1907, 598.

Biographies

Alphabetical listing

ALBRIGHT, Charles A. — **L/Corporal**
24th Bn — **WWI**

Charles Albert Albright was born on July 22nd 1897, in St-Andrews East, son of Martin William and Thirza Emily Wethey. As his father, he was also a farmer when he enlisted into the Canadian Expeditionary Force on January 17th 1916, and joined the ranks of "C" Company, 148th Overseas Battalion. He was the first of two sons to enlist, as his older brother Ewen William, was drafted in 1918 but never went overseas. Charles Albert left Canada on September 27th 1916, and arrived in England on October 6th. Once in England, he was assigned to the 24th Battalion and crossed into France on the 29th of November, to join his unit. On October 20th 1917, he was promoted to Lance/Corporal. L/Cpl Albright was killed in action on November 6th 1917, during the attack of the Canadian Corps at Passchendaele. He was buried in Plot I, Row C, Grave 34 in the Potijze Chateau Grounds Cemetery in Ieper, West-Vlaanderen, Belgium.

Service number: 841198

Medals and Awards: British War Medal and Victory Medal (1914-1919)

ANDERSON, Frank — **L/Corporal**
C.F.C. — **WWII**

Frank Anderson was born in Tawatinaw, Alberta on May 3rd 1917, son of Steve and Clena Anderson. Frank's parents were born and married in Austria and later immigrated to Canada, settling in Alberta. He didn't attend school very long, leaving at the age of nine. He worked as a farm hand for seven years then, for two years, he was employed by H.G. O'Connell Ltd out of Montreal as a steel fitter. On August 6th 1940, Frank enlisted with No.2 Company, Canadian Forestry Corps, Canadian Army, in Westmount, Quebec. At the time of his enlistment, he reported residing in Pointe-au-Chêne and being a bushman and truck driver by trade. Frank's family had remained in Alberta. From Westmount he proceeded to Valcartier, Quebec and remained with No.2 Company until February 5th 1941, when he was posted to No.9 Company also in Valcartier. He remained in Canada until April 5th, when he boarded a troopship and left Halifax, Nova Scotia arriving safely in the United Kingdom, disembarking at Gourock, Scotland on the 20th. On May 9th, he was transferred back to No.2 Company in Ballogie Camp, Scotland. On October 3rd 1941, Pte Anderson married Charlotte Kelly in the city of Edinburgh, Scotland and on the 23rd, was promoted to Lance Corporal. On March 4th 1942, while on his way to work at Ballogie Camp, L/Cpl Frank Anderson was critically injured when he fell off a truck he was a passenger in and fractured his skull. He died the next day at the Royal Infirmary in Aberdeen, Scotland. On March 11th, he was buried in Plot XXXVI, Row G, Grave 7, Brookwood Military Cemetery, Surrey, United Kingdom.

Service number: D110254

Medals and Awards: Defence Medal, the Canadian Volunteer Service Medal and clasp and the War Medal 1939-45.

ANDERSON, Norman T. **R.C.A.F.** | **Sergeant** **WWII**

LAC/BAC

Norman Thomas Anderson was born in Lachute on February 8th 1921, son of Robert Lawrence, a railway conductor and May Elizabeth Anderson. Norman grew up in Lachute, having attended the Lachute Public School from Grades 1 to 9, until June 1940. After school, he began working as a mechanic's helper with his uncle George Young Deacon. By 1941, both his parents were deceased. On July 11th 1941, Norman enlisted with the R.C.A.F. in Ottawa and was assigned to No.1 Manning Depot in Toronto immediately upon his enlistment. On September 28th, he was transferred to No.4 Wireless School in Guelph, Ontario until November 14th, when he was transferred to the Composite Training School in Trenton, Ontario. On December 9th, his training continued and was transferred to No.6 Bombing and Gunnery School in Mountain View, Ontario. He remained in Canada until he was assigned to No.1 Transit Depot in Halifax, Nova Scotia on March 4th 1943, awaiting his transport to England and the War. He boarded a troopship on the 27th, arriving safely in the United Kingdom on April 4th. On April 16th, he was assigned to No.408 Squadron in Leeming, and on October 21st, he was transferred to No.431 Squadron at R.A.F. Tholthorpe. At 2338hrs on December 3rd 1943, Sgt Anderson, a wireless operator air gunner (WOAG) was member of a crew who took off from Tholthorpe in a Halifax bomber number LK968 SE-P en route for a bombing mission. This aircraft was part of a massive 527 bomber raid in which Leipzig, Germany, was the primary target.

His bomber crashed near Hannover. Sgt Anderson and two other members of the crew were killed. The other four were taken prisoner. Norman Thomas Anderson was buried in Plot 6, Row A, Grave 16 Hanover War Cemetery, Niedersachsen, Germany.

Service number: R111471

Medals and Awards: 1939-45 Star, Air Crew Europe Star, the Canadian Volunteer Service Medal and clasp and the War Medal 1939-45.

BALDWIN, Joseph E. **Private**
R.C.A.S.C. **WWII**

Joseph Edward Baldwin was born in Morin Heights on January 14th 1916, son of James, a farmer, and Elizabeth Watson. He attended seven years of public schooling before he left at the age of 19. After school, he worked for four years as a stone cutter and 14 weeks for the Canadian National Railways as a sorter of material. Joseph Edward enlisted in the Canadian Army on April 8th 1942, in Montreal and was taken on strength with No.4 District Depot. He remained with the 4th until May 16th, when he was sent to No.41 Basic Training Centre in Huntingdon, Quebec. He was then transferred to No.A19 Royal Canadian Army Service Corps Training Centre at Camp Borden on March 10th 1943. His stay in Canada came to an end when, on July 22nd, he boarded a troopship and sailed across the Atlantic and arrived safely in the United Kingdom on the 28th, being assigned to the 84th Company, 2nd Canadian Armoured Brigade. On June 6th 1944, at approximately 12 noon, during the Normandy invasion, Pte Baldwin was in troopship MT2 Sambut when this ship was hit by a German shell fire and set on fire. Witnesses reported that the order to abandon ship had been given and that Pte Baldwin had not been wounded by the shell fire but was never seen neither reaching the water nor getting picked up by a rescue craft. Pte Joseph Edward Baldwin was never found and is commemorated on Panel 27, Column 2, Bayeux Memorial, Calvados, France.

Service number: D135077

Medals and Awards: 1939-45 Star, France and Germany Star, Defence Medal, the Canadian Volunteer Service Medal and clasp and the War Medal 1939-45.

BARKER, Hubert P. **Private**
14th Bn **WWI**

Hubert Peter Barker was born on the 25th of November 1895, in Dalesville, Chatham Township, the son of Charles William, a farmer and Jane Cruise. His father, Charles, had recently emigrated from England and had arrived in Canada around 1880. Prior to enlisting in the Canadian Expeditionary Force, Hubert had served in the 17th Duke of York's Royal Canadian Hussars, a Militia unit. On March 5th 1916, he enlisted in the 148th Overseas Battalion, for the duration of the War. He sailed from Halifax en route to England on September 26th on board the transport ship S.S. Laconia and landed on October 6th. On December 14th, he reached Continental Europe and the Western Front and joined up with his new unit, the 14th Battalion, Royal Montreal Rifles. Pte Barker was gassed on September 21st 1917, and had to be invalidated back to England at the Reading War Hospital to recuperate from the poison gas. He remained in England until April 7th 1918, when he returned to the 14th Battalion. On September 27th, Pte Barker was taking part in the attack at Bourlon Wood, which was part of the Operation aimed at breaking through the Canal-du-Nord when he suffered a gunshot wound to his left thigh and died as a result at No.33 Casualty Clearing Station on the same day. He was buried in Plot IV, Row A, Grave 13 in the Bucquoy Road Cemetery, Ficheux, Pas-de-Calais, France.

Service number: 841693

Medals and Awards: Military Medal, British War Medal and Victory Medal (1914-1919)

BELAIR, Gaëtan **L/Corporal**
Régt Chaudière **WWII**

Joseph Gaëtan Bélair was born in Brownsburg on December 14th 1919, son of Zoël and Anna Leblanc. Gaëtan grew up in Lachute having attended English and French schools. He left school at 16 years old and worked at Ayers Limited as a weaver prior to his enlistment. Gaëtan enlisted in the Canadian Army on June 25th 1943, in Montreal and upon enlistment, he was assigned to No.4 District Depot until July 15th, when he was transferred to the Basic Training Centre in St-Jérôme. On August 5th, he was sent to the Training Centre in Valleyfield to continue his training. Once his training in Canada completed, he was sent to No.1 Transit Camp in Windsor, Nova Scotia, awaiting his transport to England. He left Canada on September 14th, and reached England safely on the 19th where he was assigned to No.6 Canadian Infantry Reinforcement Unit, Algonquin Camp, Witley, England, awaiting his transfer to a combat unit. On November 4th 1943, he was transferred to the Régiment de la Chaudière, 5th Canadian Infantry Brigade, 2nd Canadian Division. This regiment was to take part in the Normandy invasion in the upcoming year. On June 6th 1944, Pte Bélair, with his regiment, landed on the shores of Normandy at Juno Beach. The invasion of Europe had started and the 2nd Canadian Division landed on the first day of the attack. Pte Bélair survived the initial landings and was promoted to Lance Corporal on July 15th. Sadly, on July 23rd, L/Cpl Joseph Gaëtan Bélair was killed in action in the vicinity of Le Poirier, France. He was buried in Colombelles, France at that time. He was later exhumed and reburied in Plot 20, Row C, Grave 16, Bretteville-sur-Laize Canadian Military Cemetery, France.

Service number: D141221

Medals and Awards: 1939-45 Star, France and Germany Star, Defence Medal, the Canadian Volunteer Service Medal and clasp and the War Medal 1939-45.

BELANGER, Gérard **Private**
R22eR **WWII**

Joseph Gérard Bélanger was born in Montreal, on January 23rd 1924, son of Rosario and Aldena Paquette. Gérard lived in Montreal for the first five years of his life until he and his family moved to Brownsburg. He attended public school until the age of 15. In 1941, he began working at the Ste-Anne Hotel as a bartender in Brownsburg. Prior to 1941, he had occupied other employments, like pin boy in a bowling alley, labourer in a toothbrush factory and servant in a grill. Prior to his enlistment, he also worked at the ammunition plant in Brownsburg. On June 29th 1942, Gérard enlisted with the Canadian Army in Montreal, and was immediately taken on strength with No.4 District Depot. On July 17th he was sent to No.44 Basic Training Centre in St-Jerome, Quebec. From there, on May 13th 1943, he was sent to No.114 Canadian Signal Training Centre in Kingston, Ontario. He attended other Signal Training Centres until August 28th, when he left Canada and sailed for the United Kingdom. He arrived safely on September 1st, and, on the next day, was assigned to No.1 Canadian Signals Reinforcement Unit. On October 15th, he was posted to the The Black Watch (Royal Highland Regiment) of Canada until January 17th 1944, when he returned to the Signals Reinforcement Unit. On May 4th, he boarded a troopship and began the perilous trip to Italy which he reached safely on the 16th, and joined his new unit, the Royal 22e Régiment. On September 20th 1944, Pte Joseph Gérard Bélanger was killed in action. On the 22nd, he was temporarily buried in the Lorenzo cemetery and was later exhumed and reburied in Plot XIV, Row G, Grave 7, Coriano Ridge War Cemetery, Italy.

Service number: D129376

Medals and Awards: 1939-45 Star, Italy Star, Defence Medal, the Canadian Volunteer Service Medal and clasp and the War Medal 1939-45.

BENETTE, James R. **Private**
P.P.C.L.I. **WWI**

James Russell Benette was born on June 28th 1895, in Chatham Township, son of Daniel, a farmer and Lilly MacDonald. Russell's mother died when he was barely four years old and his father passed away in 1905. He was left residing with his maternal grandparents, John and Cecillia MacDonald. James Russell was a teamster by trade. He enlisted in the Canadian Expeditionary Force on June 11th 1915, and joined the ranks of the Princess Patricia's Canadian Light Infantry 2nd McGill Company. Prior to his enlistment, he had served two years with the 17th Duke of York's Royal Canadian Hussars. On June 29th, he boarded the troopship S.S. Nordland and crossed to Great-Britain. He remained in England until he arrived in Rouen, France on August 24th. Sometime between June 2nd and 4th 1916, he was reported missing when the P.P.C.L.I. was hit hard by enemy artillery and assaulted by infantry while defending Sanctuary Wood in the Ypres Sector, Belgium. His body was never found. Pte Benette is commemorated on the Menin Gate Memorial in Ieper, West-Vlaanderen, Belgium.

Service number: MCG182

Medals and Awards: 1914-1915 Star, British War Medal and Victory Medal (1914-1919)

BENNETT, Robert L.B. **Private**
R.H.R. **WWII**

Robert Leslie Borden Bennett was born in Arundel on October 16th 1918, son of William George, a farmer, and Sarah Beaven. He attended public school until grade six. He worked as a farmer for a couple of years, and then was employed by the Canadian Refractories Limited in Kilmar, Quebec as a labourer. On April 21st 1941, he enrolled under the authority of the National Resources Mobilization Act and was sent to No.41 Basic Training Centre in Huntingdon, Quebec. At the time of his enrollment, he reported residing in Weir and was a miner by trade. On September 1st, he was sent to No.A2 Advanced Training Centre in Petawawa, Ontario for further training. From Petawawa, he was sent to Sydney, Nova Scotia, and joined the 9th Searchlight Battery on October 28th. Pte Bennett had discipline issues in the military. As recorded in his service file, he had been sentenced to several periods of detention for being absent without leave, escaping custody and insubordination. On August 19th 1942, he enlisted in the Canadian Active Service Force in Sydney, hence joining the active Canadian Army and remaining with the same unit. He spent the next months being assigned to coastal artillery units. He re-mustered into the infantry on February 12th 1944, and was sent to No.48 Basic Training Centre in St-Johns, Quebec the next day. He remained in St-Johns until March 12th, when he was sent to No.A12 Canadian Infantry Training Centre in Farnham, Quebec. His training lasted until June 2nd, when he boarded a troopship and left Canada for the United Kingdom, arriving safely on the 11th and proceeding to No.4 Canadian Infantry Reinforcement Unit in Helmsley, England. He was posted to the The Black Watch (Royal Highland Regiment) of Canada on June 30th, and crossed into France on July 14th. On July 25th 1944, the Royal Highlanders of Canada took part in a disastrous attack at May-Sur-Orne, France. It was during this attack that Pte Robert Leslie Borden Bennett was killed in action. He was temporarily buried in Plot 2, Row 4, Grave 11, Saint-Martin-de-Fontenay cemetery on August 13th. He was later exhumed and re-burried in Plot I, Row D, Grave 4, Bretteville-Sur-Laize Canadian War Cemetery, Calvados, France.

Service number: D135129

Medals and Awards: 1939-45 Star, France and Germany Star, the Canadian Volunteer Service Medal and clasp and the War Medal 1939-45.

BIGLOW, Percy M. **Sergeant**
1st S.S.F. **WWII**

Percy Malcolm Biglow was born in Grenville on August 17th 1921, son of Frederick and Christina Dodd. Percy attended public school for seven years, leaving at the age of 15. In 1939, he began employment with Canadian Refractories Ltd in Kilmar as a mining labourer. On August 28th 1940, he enlisted with the Canadian Army in Montreal. At that time, he reported residing in Kilmar. He was immediately taken on strength with the Victoria Rifles of Canada also in Montreal. On December 20th, he was sent to St-John's Newfoundland until October 2nd 1941, when the Victoria Rifles were sent to Valcartier, Quebec, and Rifleman Biglow followed. From Valcartier, he was sent to Nanaimo, British Columbia and on August 29th 1942, he was transferred to the 2nd Parachute Battalion with which he qualified as a paratrooper on September 11th. On April 15th 1943, Percy was sent to Norfolk, Virginia and by July 9th, found himself in San Francisco, California. On July 20th, he was promoted to acting sergeant and on the 24th, was sent to Amchitka, Alaska as part of an American Force aimed at re-capturing islands held by the Japanese. He remained until August 22nd, when he left Amchitka bound for San Francisco. This time he was part of the 1st Canadian Special Service Battalion and arrived safely on the 1st of September. He remained in the United States until October 27th, when he left the U.S. from Newport News, Virginia and arrived in Casablanca, Morocco on November 5th. The 1st S.S.F. made its way to the port of Oran, Algeria where Sgt Biglow boarded another ship and crossed the Mediterranean and disembarked in Naples, Italy on November 13th. On December 5th 1943, Sgt Biglow was killed in the vicinity of Mt. La Defensa, Italy. He was buried in the Canadian

Plot, Grave 12, in the temporary U.S. Military Cemetery at Mt La Defensa. He was later exhumed, a first time, being reburied in Plot AA, Row 3, Grave 31, in the American Military Cemetery in Frattelle, Italy. He was then exhumed again and reburied in Plot IV, Row F, Grave 5, Cassino War Cemetery, Italy.

Service number: D71806

Medals and Awards: 1939-45 Star, Italy Star, the Canadian Volunteer Service Medal and clasp and the War Medal 1939-45.

BIGROW, Johnny E. **Private**
1st Quebec Regt **WWI**

Johnny Edward Bigrow was born on the 28th of August 1894, in Arundel, son of John, a farmer, and Margaret McClusky. Johnny was a farmer like his father. He was conscripted into the 1st Depot Battalion of the 1st Quebec Regiment, Canadian Expeditionary Force on August 22nd 1918. He never made it overseas. Johnny died on Oct 30th 1918, of influenza and was buried in the Arundel Anglican cemetery.

Service number: 3091266

Medals and Awards: None

BLANCHARD, Evariste **Private**
13th Bn **WWI**

Joseph Eugène Evariste Blanchard was born on January 28th 1896, in St-Henri, Montreal, son of Georges, a machinist, and Victorine Beauvais. Evariste's mother died a few months after his birth. His father Georges remarried in 1902 to

Cordélie Mitchell from Longueuil, Quebec. The family remained in Montreal until they moved to St-Jean, Quebec sometime prior to September 1914. By 1921, Evariste's father had moved to Brownsburg, Quebec. Evariste was a box maker by trade and had served with the 85th Regiment, a Montreal based militia unit for approximately one year prior to his enlistment. He volunteered to join the Canadian Expeditionary Force on September 23rd 1914, when he joined the 13th Battalion, The Royal Highlanders of Canada. He sailed for Great-Britain on board the S.S. Alaunia on October 3rd, disembarking on the 15th. After a period of training, he boarded another ship and crossed the Channel, landing in St-Nazaire, France, on February 15th 1915. On May 20th, during an operation at Festubert France, by Canadian units including the 13th Battalion, it had been reported that Pte Blanchard had been wounded and needed stretcher bearers to retrieve him. Unfortunately, this information had been relayed by another soldier who was also killed during the battle. Evariste Blanchard's body was never found. He is commemorated on the Menin Gate Memorial in Ieper, West-Vlaanderen, Belgium.

Service number: 24337

Medals and Awards: 1914-1915 Star, British War Medal and Victory Medal (1914-1919)

BOA, Frank T. — **Private**
14th Bn — **WWI**

Frank Tracy Boa was born on August 10th 1896, in Montreal, Quebec, son of Thomas and Emily Burgin. By 1911, this family was residing in Lachute. He enlisted with the 148th Overseas Battalion on January 25th 1916. Frank was the second son to enlist as he followed in his older brother's, Archibald, footsteps. Andrew John a third brother was to enlist in 1918. Both Archibald and Andrew John survived the War. On September 27th, Frank sailed for Great-Britain on board the troopship S.S. Laconia and landed in England on October 6th. He was transferred to the 14th Battalion on December 13th, and arrived in France the next day where he joined his Battalion in the Trenches at Berthonval. On August 9th 1918, Pte Boa was killed in action during his Battalion's attack in the vicinity of Warvillers, France. He has no known grave and is commemorated on the Vimy Memorial, Pas-de-Calais, France.

Service number: 841235

Medals and Awards: British War Medal and Victory Medal (1914-1919)

BOYD, Benjamin W. **Private**
49th Bn **WWI**

Benjamin Wellington Boyd was born in Arundel on August 21st 1891, son of Thomas, a farmer, and Elizabeth Moore. By the end of 1892, Benjamin's father had died and his mother had remarried in Ottawa, in 1899, to James Loudfoot. Benjamin enlisted with the 66th Overseas Battalion, Canadian Expeditionary Force on September 7th 1915, in Edmonton, Alberta. He remained in Canada until April 28th 1916, when he boarded the S.S. Olympic and crossed the Atlantic, reaching the United Kingdom safely on May 7th. On June 6th, he was transferred to the 49th Battalion, landed in France two days later, and joined his new Battalion in the trenches. Pte Boyd was involved rapidly in action as he was wounded on August 18th, and removed from the lines, evacuated to No.15 Casualty Clearing Station and treated for a gunshot wound to his left thumb. He returned to his unit on the 23rd. On October 8-9th 1916, the 49th Battalion launched an attack on the Regina Trench in order to dislodge the Germans from the trenches. This attack met fierce ennemy resistance and Pte Benjamin Wellington Boyd was killed during this action. The war diarist reported that the 49th suffered 221 casualties out of a starting strength of 463. Pte Boyd has no known grave and is commemorated on the Vimy Memorial, Pas-de-Calais, France.

Service number: 101246

Medals and Awards: British War Medal and Victory Medal (1914-1919)

BOYD, George D. **F/Officer**
R.C.A.F. **WWII**

LAC/BAC

George Daniel Boyd was born in Dalesville on September 15th 1922, son of Austin George, a carpenter, and Evelyn Myrtle Lalanne. George remained in Chatham Township throughout his childhood, having attended school in Brownsburg. After school, he was employed as an apprentice toolmaker with the Canadian Industries Limited company in Brownsburg. On July 16th 1941, he enlisted in the R.C.A.F. in Montreal and was immediately assigned to No.4 Manning Depot in St-Hubert until August 29th, when he was assigned to No.3 Training Centre. Followed were several training assignments which culminated with him attending No.1 Bombing and Gunnery School in Jarvis, Ontario, on March 29th 1942. On May 17th, he was transferred to No.31 Operational Training Unit in Debert, Nova Scotia. On July 1st, he was transferred to the Royal Air Force Ferry Command. As such, on April 1st 1943, he was posted to Nassau, Bahamas, with No.113 South Atlantic Wing, Royal Air Force. Having been promoted to Warrant Officer II by April 27th, he was commissioned an officer and promoted to the rank of Pilot Officer on July 14th. On January 14th 1944, he was again promoted, this time to the rank of Flying Officer. F/O Boyd was assigned to No.45 (Atlantic Transport) Group, Royal Air Force in Dorval, Quebec. On November 12th 1944, he was the wireless operator on a Mosquito aircraft number KB.504, which had left Gander, Newfoundland enroute to the United Kingdom via Greenland. Normal radio contact was kept with this aircraft until an S.O.S. was received from Gander which was presumed to have originated from F/O Boyd's aircraft. An air sea rescue was initiated but failed to locate the aircraft, F/O Boyd or the civilian pilot. F/O George Daniel Boyd was lost at sea and his body was never recovered. He is commemorated on the Ottawa Memorial, Ottawa, Ontario.

Service number: J29634

Medals and Awards: 1939-45 Star, Atlantic Star, the Canadian Volunteer Service Medal and clasp and the War Medal 1939-45.

BOYD, Oswald R. **Private**
R.H.R. **WWII**

Oswald Raymond Boyd was born in Dalesville on June 19th 1903, son of William John and Margret

Ellen Dixon. Oswald remained with his parents in Chatham Twp all his life and worked as a clerk prior to his enlistment. He enlisted with the Canadian Army on November 29th 1939, in Montreal. He was immediately posted to the 1st Battalion, The Black Watch (Royal Highland Regiment) of Canada. He remained in Canada until June 17th 1940, when he boarded the Antonia and landed safely on the 22nd in Botwood, Newfoundland. He remained in Newfoundland until August 10th, when he boarded the troopship S.S. Duchess of Richmond. He returned to Canada landing on the 13th, in Halifax and proceeded to the Infantry Training Centre in Aldershot, Nova Scotia. On August 22nd, he boarded an EC2 class troopship and left Canada for the United Kingdom and landed safely in Gourrock, Scotland on September 4th. While in the United Kingdom, he was assigned to different units. On November 7th 1942, he was admitted to the Royal Infirmary in Glasgow Scotland, having suffered a perforated gastric ulcer. Pte Boyd was operated on but at 1300hrs on November 12th, he died of post-operative pneumonia. He was buried on November 18th, in Plot 33, Row H, Grave 4 Brookwood Military Cemetery, Surrey, United Kingdom.

Service number: D81871

Medals and Awards: Defence Medal, the Canadian Volunteer Service Medal and clasp and the War Medal 1939-45.

BOYD, Walter D.C. **F/Officer**
R.C.A.F. **WWII**

LAC/BAC

Walter Dawson Carl Boyd was born in Arundel on January 17th 1921, son of Harry, a farmer and Louisa Beattie. He attended the Arundel Intermediate School from 1927 to 1939 and then the Lachute High School from 1939 to 1940. He was employed, from August to December 1940, at the Canadian Industries Limited. Afterwards he was employed at the F.H. Wheeler Hotel in St-Jovite, Quebec as a hotel desk clerk. On March 6th 1941, he enlisted with the Royal Canadian Air Force, aspiring to be a pilot, in Montreal. On the 14th, he was taken on strength with No.1 Manning Depot in Toronto. On June 22nd, he was sent to No.1 Initial Training School also in Toronto. His flight training had started. On July 26th, he was sent to No.11 Elementary Flying Training School in Cap de la Madeleine, Quebec. On September 14th, he was sent to No.8 Service Flying Training School in Moncton, New-Brunswick for further flight training. He remained in Canada, undergoing further training until he was sent to Europe on February 9th 1942, arriving safely on the 19th, and was sent to Bournemouth, England and assigned to No.3 Personnel Reception Centre. He underwent further training, being assigned to No.2 Advance Flying Unit and No.7 Operational Training Unit. He was sent to the Middle East on December 9th 1942, and was transferred to 38 Squadron R.A.F. on January 8th 1943. Walter was commissioned an officer in the R.A.F., on July 3rd. On the night of the 1st of March 1944, Flying Officer Boyd was the pilot of a Wellington Mk XIII bomber number MP.742 which had been detailed to a shipping strike in the Aegean Sea and the bombing of Melos, Greece as an alternate target. The aircraft took off from RAF Berka III airfield in Lybia. This was the last time the aircraft or the crew were seen. It was assumed that all lost their lives at sea. Flying Officer Walter Dawson Carl Boyd is remembered on Panel 281, Alamein Memorial, Egypt.

Service number: J18761

Medals and Awards: 1939-45 Star, Africa Star, Defence Medal, the Canadian Volunteer Service Medal and clasp and the War Medal 1939-45.

BRADFORD, Reuben C. **L/Corporal**
P.P.C.L.I. **WWI**

Reuben Carman Bradford was born on October 22nd 1896, in the Township of Chatham, son of William Henry, a farmer, and Isabella Rogers. On June 19th 1915, he enlisted with the 2nd McGill Company, Princess Patricia's Canadian Light Infantry, one month after his older brother, William Cecil, had enlisted in the 38th Battalion. Reuben had 12 months prior military service, having served with the 17th Duke of York's Royal Canadian Hussars. On June 29th, he boarded the troopship S.S. Nordland and reported to the 11th Battalion in Shorncliffe, England on July 18th. One month later, on August 24th, he landed in France and joined his Battalion. He was severely wounded on December 19th, while in the trenches in the vicinity of La Folie, France and died the next day at No.42 Casualty Clearing Station of a gunshot wound to the head. He was buried in Plot I, Row F, Grave 20 in the Aubigny Communal Cemetery Extension, Pas-de-Calais, France.

Service Number: MCG222

Medals and Awards: 1914-1915 Star, British War Medal and Victory Medal (1914-1919)

BRUNELLE, Paul **Private**
Algonquin Regt. **WWII**

Courtesy The Watchman 1944

Joseph Hilaire Léopold Gilles (Paul) Brunelle was born in Montreal on September 30th 1925, son of Ernest and Jeannette Therrien. He resided in Montreal for the first four years of his life then, him and his family, moved to Arundel and Lost River. He attended Public School until completing Grade seven at age 14. On October 7th 1943, he enlisted with the Canadian Army in Kingston, Ontario and assigned to No.3A District Depot. At the time of his enlistment, he reported working at Ayers Limited in Carling Lake as a truck driver and residing in Lost River. His brother George would also enlist in the Canadian Army. He survived the War. Paul was sent to No.60 Basic Training Camp, in Yarmouth, Nova Scotia on October 22nd. He remained in Yarmouth until December 18th, when he was sent to No.A14 Canadian Infantry Training Centre in Aldershot, Nova Scotia. His training was well under way. From Aldershot, he was sent to No.S17 Canadian School of Infantry in Vernon, British Columbia, on January 27th 1944. He remained in Canada until December 18th, when he boarded a troopship and landed safely in England on Christmas Day 1944, being assigned to No.3 Canadian Infantry Training Regiment in Aldershot. On February 24th 1945, he arrived in Continental Europe and on March 7th joined his unit, the Algonquin Regiment. On April 18th 1945, the Algonquin

Regiment was engaged in a sharp battle with the Germans in the vicinity of the Kusten Kanal, Germany. Pte Paul Brunelle was killed during this action. He was temporarily buried in the Freisoythe cemetery in Germany until he was exhumed and reburied in Plot VII, Row D, Grave 11, Holten Canadian War Cemetery, Overijssel, Holland.

Service number: C122538

Medals and Awards: 1939-45 Star, France and Germany Star, the Canadian Volunteer Service Medal and clasp and the War Medal 1939-45.

BUCHAN, William E. **Lieutenant**
R.F.C. **WWI**

William Erskine Buchan was born in Montreal, on July 31st 1898, the son of prominent lawyer John Stuart Buchan, originally from St-Andrews East, and Annie Henderson. When William Erskine was 2, his father published "A bit of Atlantis", a novel under the pseudonym Douglas Erskine. William Erskine was commissioned in the Royal Flying Corps, the predecessor of the Royal Air Force, on November 27th 1917. He joined No.93 Squadron at Chattis Hill, England and was confirmed in the rank of Flying Officer on January 15th 1918. Sadly, he was killed in an airplane accident on March 9th 1918, when the aircraft he was flying, a S.E. 5 fighter number 8277, stalled when making a turn near the ground. A Court of Inquiry concluded that this accident was a result of pilot error. William Erskine Buchan was buried in the Stockbridge cemetery, Hampshire, England.
Service number: Lieutenant

Medal and Awards: British War Medal

BURNS, Richard **Private**
75th Bn **WWI**

Richard Burns was born on January 30th 1887 in Lakeview, Harrington Township, the son of Henry, a farmer, and Mary Cameron. Richard's mother died when he was 12 years old and his father passed away in 1901. By 1911, he was the head of the family, residing with two sisters and his younger brother William in Harrington. William enlisted in the Canadian Expeditionary Force on April 10th 1916, and joined the 119th Battalion. William survived the War and died in 1963. Richard was drafted on April 19th 1918 and at the time, was residing in Monetville, Ontario. He left Canada on June 3rd 1918, and arrived in England on the 21st on board the troopship S.S. Cassandra. On his arrival, he was assigned to the 12th Reserve Battalion, and on the 28th of September was assigned to "D" Company, 75th Battalion. He was seriously wounded on November 4th, during an attack by the Battalion at a road between Rombies and Quaroble France, having received a gunshot wound to his chest and spine. He was evacuated to England and his wound left him in a complete state of paraplegia. Richard Burns died of his wounds on February 5th 1919, at Bevan Military Hospital, Sandgate, England. He was buried in Plot U, Grave 731 in the Shorncliffe Military Cemetery, Kent, England.

Service number: 3035147

Medals and Awards: British War Medal and Victory Medal (1914-1919)

BURNS, Stephen W. **Corporal**
P.P.C.L.I. **WWI**

William Joseph Stephen Burns was born in Grenville, on January 13th 1890, son of James, a butcher, and Margaret Matthews. Both of his parents had died by 1911. Stephen William relocated to Edmonton Alberta, where he had militia service with the 101st Edmonton Fusiliers and worked as an accountant. When World War One erupted he quickly enlisted with No.2 Company, Princess Patricia's Canadian Light Infantry on August 25th 1914, in Ottawa Ontario. He sailed for Great-Britain on October 4th on board the troopship S.S. Royal George. He remained in England until he left Southampton for France on December 20th. He was promoted to Corporal on March 6th, 1915. On the same day, while in the trenches at Dickebush, Belgium, his trench was hit by German artillery fire. He was seriously wounded by shrapnel to his head and legs and transported to No.8 Casualty Clearing Station. Corporal Stephen William Burns died that same day at 1710hrs. He was buried in Plot J, Grave 19, in the Bailleul Communal Cemetery, Nord, France.

Service number: 518

Medals and Awards: 1914-1915 Star, British War Medal and Victory Medal (1914-1919)

BUTLER, Charles A. **Private**
24th Bn **WWI**

Charles Andrew Butler was born in Ottawa Ontario, on December 27th 1897, the son of Charles William, a salesman, and Rosanna McCullough. He resided with his parents on Glen Avenue in Ottawa. By 1916, he was residing in

Brownsburg. On March 25th 1916, Charles Andrew, as many others from the area did, enlisted into "C" Company, 148th Overseas Battalion, in Lachute. He left Canada on September 27th, and crossed overseas on board the troopship S.S. Laconia, arriving in Liverpool England, on October 6th. On November 28th, he was transferred to the 24th Battalion and arrived in France the next day. Charles Andrew Butler was killed in action during the Canadian attack at Vimy Ridge on April 9th 1917. He was 19 years old. He was buried in Plot II, Row B, Grave 9, in the Thelus Military Cemetery, Pas-de-Calais, France.

Service number: 841897

Medals and Awards: British War Medal and Victory Medal (1914-1919)

CALDER, William M. C.F.C. **Captain WWI**

McGill Honour Roll 1914-1918

William McClure Calder was born in Lachute, on October 6th 1894, son of George and Jemima Rogers. William McClure was the first of two brothers to enlist in the Canadian Army during World War One. His older brother, John Rodger, enlisted in April 1918 as a physician. In 1914, William McClure enrolled at McGill University in Montreal as an Arts student. He enlisted as a Private with the 1st Universities Company, P.P.C.L.I. on the 6th of April 1915. He crossed overseas on the 29th of May on board the troopship S.S. Northland. He remained in England until he arrived in France and joined his unit on July 17th. In October, he became ill and was diagnosed with appendicitis and was admitted to several hospitals in England. He was finally discharged from the hospital on April 19th 1916. He remained in England until the 15th of September, when he was returned to Canada to be discharged as an enlisted man and commissioned into the Canadian Expeditionary Force, 242nd Battalion. After his appointment, he, once again, crossed the Atlantic on November 23rd, on board the troopship H.M.T. Mauritania and returned to England for further service, this time as a Lieutenant, disembarking on the 30th in Liverpool. He was transferred from the 242nd Battalion to No.22 Company, Canadian Forestry Corps and landed in France on February 4th 1917. Two and a half months later, on April 19th, William McClure was again transferred. This time it was to No.5 District Headquarters, Canadian Forestry Corps. He was promoted to the rank of Honorary Captain and assigned to be Quartermaster on July 1st, Canada`s Confederation Day. Capt Calder survived the horrors of battle but sadly, on November 1st 1918, just 10 days prior to the Armistice, he was killed in a motorcycle accident. A Court of Inquiry was assembled on November 5th which revealed that at approximately 1715hrs on November 1st, Capt Calder was operating a motorcycle on the road in the vicinity of Censeau, France and collided with a transport lorry head on. He was taken to La Joux Hospital where his death was confirmed. There was no blame assigned to the lorry driver. Capt Calder was buried with full military honours on November 4th 1918, in Row B Grave 4, Champagnol Communal Cemetery, Jura, France.

Service number: 411031

Medals and Awards: 1914-1915 Star, British War Medal and Victory Medal (1914-1919)

CAMPBELL, Douglas J. **Private**
1st Sask. Regt **WWI**

Douglas John Campbell was born in Mille-Isles, on May 21st 1893, son of Thomas and Mary Riddell. His father had emigrated from Ireland and was a blacksmith. Thomas passed away in 1893. In 1901, Douglas John was residing with his grandfather William Riddell in Mille-Iles and in 1911 with his uncle Hugh Riddell. He was drafted under the Military Services Act of 1917 on November 11th 1917, and defaulted. He was apprehended on July 17th 1918, and at that time resided in Regina, Saskatchewan. On the 23rd of January 1919, he died of pneumonia while on harvest leave in Grenfell, Saskatchewan. He was buried in the Mille-Isles Presbyterian Cemetery.

Service number: 3355525

Medals and Awards: Nil

CAMPBELL, Malcolm **Private**
R.W.R. **WWII**

Malcolm George Campbell (né Elder) was born in Montreal on January 25th 1918, son of Walter Elder, a farmer in the parish of St-Sauveur, and Marion Doherty. Malcolm's mother died two days after his birth and was buried in the Mille Isles cemetery. Malcolm became the foster child of Samuel Campbell and his wife Annie Sutton from his infancy and always used the surname of Campbell thereafter. The Campbells were from the Mille Isles area and by 1935 they were residing in Morin Heights. He attended public school for seven years and left at the age of 15. Malcolm's foster parents died in 1938. Prior to his enlistment, he had worked as a truck driver and owned a farm in Mille Isles. On January 28th 1943, Malcolm enlisted in the Canadian Army in Montreal and was taken on strength with No.4 District Depot until February 13th, when he was sent to No.41 Basic Training Centre in Huntingdon, Quebec. On April 30th, he was then sent to No.A12 Canadian Infantry Training Centre in Farnham, Quebec to continue his training. He remained in Canada until December 14th, when he left Canada, crossed the Atlantic and disembarked safely in the United Kingdom on the 21st. The next day, he was taken on strength with No.5 Canadian Infantry Reinforcement Unit at Tourney Barracks, England to, yet again, undergo further infantry training. On March 14th 1944, Pte Campbell was posted to the 1st Battalion, The Black Watch (Royal Highland Regiment) of Canada and on April 23rd, was transferred to the Royal Winnipeg Rifles. On June 6th 1944, Pte Campbell and his Battalion waded ashore on the beaches of Normandy. He remained in France, fighting with his Battalion. On July 4th, the Royal Winnipeg Rifles were ordered to attack a key German airfield at Carpiquet. It was during this attack that Pte Campbell was mortally wounded. He died the next day. Pte Malcolm Campbell was temporarily buried, in Plot 27, Grave 17, Beny-Sur-Mer Cemetery, on the 15th. He was later exhumed and reburied in Plot XIV, Row G, Grave 1, Beny-Sur-Mer Canadian War Cemetery, Reviers, Calvados, France.

Service number: D132766

Medals and Awards: 1939-45 Star, France and Germany Star, the Canadian Volunteer Service Medal and clasp and the War Medal 1939-45.

CAMPBELL, William **Private**
21st Bn **WWI**

William Edward Campbell was born on February 19th 1892, in Little Rideau, East Hawkesbury Twp, Ontario son of Daniel, a labourer, and Louisa Lamoureux. William may have been an employee at Dominion Cartridge Company of Brownsburg. He volunteered for the Canadian Expeditionary Force on April 8th 1916, joining the 154th Overseas Battalion. He left Canada on October 25th, and arrived in England six days later. Once in England, he was transferred to the 156th Battalion sometime in January 1917. On January 28th, he was again transferred to the 6th Reserve Battalion. He was finally assigned to a combat unit, the 21st Battalion, on April 21st, arriving in France on the 22nd. With the 21st, he saw combat and was wounded on March 4th 1918. William Edward Campbell was killed in action on October 11th 1918, while taking part in a military operation near Avesnes-le-Sec, France. The Battalion had suffered heavily in the first half-hour of that attack, having sustained 50% casualties in its officers, NCOs and Lewis Gunners. He was buried in Row E, Plot 1, Grave 10, Niagara Cemetery, Iwuy, Nord, France.

Service number: 634018

Medals and Awards: British War Medal and Victory Medal (1914-1919)

CARPENTER, Clifton G. **Sergeant**
1st Bn **WWI**

Clifton Gordon Carpenter was born in Montreal on July 3rd 1898, son of Silas H., a well-known and respected Chief of Detectives with the Montreal Police Department and Clara Jane Trollope. Silas was born in Brownsburg and in 1911 resided with his family in Lachute. In 1912 he became Edmonton's Chief of Police. Clifton had moved to Alberta and in 1915 resided in Banff. He enlisted with the 82nd Overseas Battalion, Canadian Expeditionary Force on November 2nd 1915 in Calgary, Alberta. In his attestation paper, his year of birth is off by one year, making him 18, but in reality he was only 17 years old when he enlisted. On May 20th 1916, he made the crossing to England on board the troopship S.S. Empress of Britain, landing on the 29th. On his arrival, he was transferred to several Reserve Battalions until he was eventually transferred to the 1st Battalion. He joined his unit in France on April 27th. On May 4th 1917, he was promoted to sergeant. On November 6th, during the horrific Battle of Passchendaele, in the vicinity of Wieltje, Belgium, Sgt Clifton Gordon Carpenter was hit by an enemy shell and instantly killed. During that battle, the 1st Battalion suffered 50% casualties as mentioned by the war diarist in his report. Sgt Carpenter's body was never found. Clifton Gordon Carpenter is commemorated on the Menin Gate Memorial in Ieper, West-Vlaanderen, Belgium.

Service number: 160986

Medals and Awards: British War Medal and Victory Medal (1914-1919)

CARTER, Herbert **Unknown**
Unknown **WWI**

Unfortunetely, this soldier could not be positively identified. He is commemorated on the Lachute and Brownsburg Memorials.

Service number: Unknown

Medals and Awards: Unknown

CHRISTIE, Edgar W. **2nd Lieutenant**
R.A.F. **WWI**

Edgar Watchorn Christie was born in Victoria, British Columbia, on January 30th 1898, the son of Gilbert David and Annie Watchorn. Gilbert David was a native of Lachute and had moved to British Columbia where he married Annie in 1896. Edgar was a clerk by trade and had served with the 5th Canadian Field Artillery and the 50th Gordon Highlanders prior to his enlistment in Victoria, on April 28th 1916, when he joined the 62nd Battery of the 15th Overseas Brigade, Canadian Field Artillery. He made the crossing to England, leaving Halifax on September 11th, on board the troopship S.S. Cameronia, and arrived in Liverpool on the 22nd. He remained in England, at first with the 15th Brigade, and then with the 14th Brigade when transferred, on January 22nd 1917. On July 21st, Edgar was sent to Denham, Buckinghamshire to take a flying course. He was discharged in London, England from the 58th Battery on October 24th 1917, in consequence of being commissionned in the Royal Flying Corps. He trained at the Central Flying School and was appointed a Flying Officer on January 2nd 1918. He was transferred to No.60 Squadron at Ste-Marie-Cappel, France flying SE.5 fighter aircrafts. On April 2nd 1918, 2nd Lt Christie took off at about 1730hrs and was assigned to an Offensive Patrol, flying aircraft B8236, a SE.5a fighter, in the vicinity of Vrély-Rosières, France when he engaged an enemy aircraft at around 1816hrs. His aircraft was shot down as reported by German sources. His aircraft and his body were never found. Edgar Watchorn Christie is commemorated on the Arras Flying Services Memorial, Pas-de-Calais, France.

Service number: 332801

Medals and Awards: British War Medal and Victory Medal (1914-1919)

CLARK, Donald K. **R.C.A.F.** **F/Sergeant** **WWII**

LAC/BAC

Donald Kenneth Clark was born in Mount Maple near Brownsburg on March 26th 1923, son of George Andrew and Jessie Wright MacKenzie. Jessie died in 1925. Donald attended Brownsburg Public School from 1929 to 1939 and then Brownsburg High School until 1942. He was employed on his brother's farm from November 1942 onwards. Donald remained on the family farm in Mount Maple all his life until he enlisted with the Royal Canadian Air Force on February 10th 1943, in Ottawa, Ontario and was immediately taken on strength with No.5 Manning Depot in Lachine, Quebec. On April 9th, he was sent to R.C.A.F. Station in Mountain View, Ontario. His stay in Mountain View was a short one. On the 19th, he was sent to No.2 Military District in Brandon, Manitoba. On June 13th, he was sent to No.3 Wireless School in Winnipeg, Manitoba. His training continued. On January 1st 1944, he was posted to No.7 Bombing and Gunnery School in Paulson, Manitoba. He remained in Canada, training with other units, until August 3rd when he sailed for the United Kingdom, arriving safely on the 10th. On arrival he was sent to No.3 Personnel Reception Centre in Bournemouth, England and on the 29th was transferred to No.223 Squadron, Royal Air Force in Oulton, England. On January 14th 1945, Flight Sgt Clark was a member of a Liberator bomber crew number TT.536, which took off from R.A.F. Oulton, on a mission to disrupt enemy radio communications and radar in the vicinity of Grevenbroich, Germany. This aircraft was seen on fire on its return leg and crashed 12 miles south-east of Antwerp. Of the eleven crew members, two survived. Flight Sgt Clark did not survive the crash and was buried in Collective Grave IV.D.9-12, Leopoldsburg War Cemetery, Limburg, Belgium.

Service number: R207938

Medals and Awards: 1939-45 Star, France and Germany Star, the Canadian Volunteer Service Medal and clasp and the War Medal 1939-45.

CLARK, William G. **F/Officer**
R.C.A.F. **WWII**

Courtesy Ruth Whetnall

William Garfield Clark was born in Lachute on May 19th 1914, son of David John, a millwright and Annie May Marshall. He attended Lachute High School from 1920 to 1931 and MacDonald College in 1931 and 1932. He worked a short period for the Gatineau School Board as a teacher and returned to Ayers Ltd in Lachute as a designer from 1933 to 1936. From 1936 until his enlistment in 1940, he was employed as a Superintendent at Johnson Woolen Mills Ltd in Waterville, Quebec. On September 24th 1940, William Garfield enlisted in the Royal Canadian Air Force. He attended No.2 Initial Training School in Regina, Saskatchewan from December 24th 1940 until January 24th 1941, where he successfully passed this class with an average of 86%. On July 12th 1941, he married Edith Jacques Rosborough in Lachute. He was then transferred to No. 16 Elemental Flying Training School in Edmonton, Alberta where he began his flying career on Tiger Moth aircrafts. Once completed, he received further advanced training at the No. 11 Service Flying Training School in Yorton, Saskatchewan where he received instructions on the Harvard aircraft. On June 14th 1941, he finished 8th in a class of 52 and received positive comments from the Chief Ground Instructor. He was then sent overseas, being assigned to No. 53 and later to No. 12 Operational Training Unit in the United Kingdom, where he received further training until being posted to No. 99 R.A.F. Bomber Squadron in Digri, India on June 5th 1942. On the night of the 4/5th January 1943, Flying Officer Clark, at the command of a Wellington bomber number HD.977, was detailed to bomb targets at the Mandalay Marshalling Yards in Burma. When the aircraft returned and landed after an apparent successful mission, an unexploded bomb, from its own bomb load, exploded directly underneath the aircraft. He was critically injured and taken to the Military Hospital in Calcutta where, on the 24th, he died as a result of these injuries. He was buried with full military honours in Plot O, Row D, Grave 8 at the Bhowanipore Cemetery, Calcutta, India.

Service number: J5972

Medals and Awards: 1939-45 Star, Burma Star, the Canadian Volunteer Service Medal and clasp and the War Medal 1939-45.

COPELAND, Thomas **Private**
44th Bn **WWI**

Thomas Copeland was born on September 17th 1886, in the Township of Gore, son of Anthony, a farmer, and Ann McKinley. Thomas' father, Anthony, died in 1908 and his mother Ann passed away in 1913. On May 6th 1915, Thomas enlisted with the 44th Overseas Battalion in Winnipeg, Manitoba. On October 22nd, he boarded the troopship S.S. Lapland in Halifax and disembarked in Bramshott, England on the 30th. He remained in England until his arrival in Le Havre, France on August 12th 1916. He spent three and a half months temporarily assigned to the 176th Tunnelers Company, Royal Engineers. He eventually returned to the 44th Battalion on April 3rd 1917, and suffered a gunshot wound to his right arm one week later. He spent some time recuperating, and on his return to the field, was assigned to the 4th Engineer Battalion until September 2nd, when he re-joined his unit, the 44th Battalion. On October 29th 1917, the 44th Battalion suffered about 50 casualties during an attack in the Passchendaele area. Thomas Copeland was seriously wounded having received shrapnel to his right thigh. Sadly he died the next day at the 3rd Australian Casualty Clearing Station. He was buried in Plot VIII, Row B, Grave 5 in the Nine Elms British Cemetery, West-Vlaanderen, Belgium.

Service number: 622933

Medals and awards: British War Medal and Victory Medal (1914-1919)

COURSOL, Eugène **Private**
10th Res Bn **WWI**

Joseph Eugène Paul Coursol was born on July 17th 1896, in Lachine Quebec, son of Damase and Julienne Therrien. Eugène was drafted into the 2nd Depot Battalion, 2nd Quebec Regiment on August 27th 1918. At that time he was residing at 5 St-Louis Street, Lachine and was an operator by trade. He boarded the troopship H.M.T. Saturnia three days later on the 30th and arrived safely in Liverpool, England on September 17th. On arrival, he proceeded to Bramshott and on the 30th, was transferred to the 10th Reserve Battalion. Eugène became ill with influenza and was admitted to No.12 Canadian General Hospital, in Bramshott, on October 24th. Eugène would lose his battle against the illness. He died on November 28th 1918, and was buried in Row C, Grave 010, Grayshott (St. Joseph) Roman Catholic Churchyard Cemetery, Hampshire, United Kingdom.

Service number: 3172631

Medals and awards: British War Medal

COUSENS, Clifford **Sapper**
R.C.E. **WWII**

Clifford John Ernest Cousens was born in Grenville Township on May 20th 1921, son of Thomas John, a farmer and Margaret Burk. Clifford grew up in Rawcliffe and attended school until the age of 16. From 1936 to 1941 he worked as a farm labourer on his parents' farm. Afterwards he started working as a miner for the Canadian Refractories Ltd company in Kilmar. On June 18th 1942, he enlisted with the Canadian Army in Ottawa and on the 27th, he was sent to

No.31 Basic Training Centre in Cornwall, Ontario. He remained in Cornwall until August 26th, when he was sent to No.A5 Canadian Engineers Training Centre in Petawawa, Ontario. His engineer training continued until December 29th, when he boarded a troopship and made the crossing to the United Kingdom, arriving safely on January 7th 1943. He was taken on strength with the Canadian Engineers Reinforcement Unit the next day. Sapper Cousens trained in the United Kingdom and was transferred to No.16 Field Company on August 11th. On June 6th 1944, Sapper Cousens was part of the invasion of France and landed on the beaches of Normandy. On October 14th, while the 16th was in the vicinity of the Leopold Canal in Belgium supporting the Canadian attack to clear the Scheldt Estuary, he was hit by shrapnel to the back of both legs and arms and was evacuated to No.2 Canadian Casualty Clearing Station. He died two days later. He was temporarily buried in Belgium and later exhumed and re-interred in Plot XI, Row C, Grave 2, Adegem Canadian War Cemetery, Oost-Vlaanderen, Belgium.

Service number: C100525

Medals and Awards: 1939-45 Star, France and Germany Star, Defence Medal, the Canadian Volunteer Service Medal and clasp and the War Medal 1939-45.

CRAIG, Norman R. **Trooper**
29th Recce **WWII**

Norman Roy Craig was born in Harrington East, on March 21st 1923, son of Godfrey and Mary Dubeau. He attended school but left at the early age of 12 in order to assist his mother, since his father had passed away in 1932. In 1937, Mary remarried with Charles David Staniforth of Arundel. In 1939, Norman began employment with the Constant Courts Company, in Rouge Valley, as a truck driver and remained with this company until his enlistment. On August 31st 1943, Norman enlisted in the Canadian Army in Montreal and was assigned to No.4 District Depot. On September 16th, he reported to No.13 Basic Training Centre in Listowell, Ontario. From Listowell, he was sent to Winnipeg for one week and, on November 13th, was assigned to No.1 Canadian Armoured Corps Training Regiment at Camp Borden, Ontario. He remained in Canada, training, until April 30th 1944, when he boarded a troopship, arriving safely in the United Kingdom on May 6th, and was assigned to No.2 Canadian Armoured Corps Reinforcement Unit at West Frith Barracks, Clackdown, Surrey. Remaining in the United Kingdom for a few months, he crossed into France on July 30th. On September 16th, he was transferred to the 29th Armoured Reconnaissance Regiment. On October 15th 1944, Trooper Norman Roy Craig was killed in action in the area of Brecht, Belgium while his unit was engaged in a sharp, small firefight with German Forces. He was buried in Plot III, Row B, Grave 18, Schoonselhof Cemetery, Antwerpen, Belgium.

Service number: D142356

Medals and Awards: 1939-45 Star, France and Germany Star, the Canadian Volunteer Service Medal and clasp and the War Medal 1939-45.

CRESSWELL, Arthur C. **Lt/Cmdr**
Royal Navy **WWII**

Arthur Clifford Cresswell was born in Renfrew, Ontario on April 27th 1899, son of John Robert, a Baptist Minister and Minnie Maud Howell. His father, John, was Minister of the Baptist Church in Lachute from 1894 until 1896. This family moved, residing in Stanstead County, Quebec in 1901, again in Lachute in 1902 and in Manitoba by 1911. Arthur Clifford attended the Lachute High School at a certain time in his life. When World War One erupted in 1914, Arthur Clifford was still in Canada. He remained until he boarded the SS Metagama in Montreal, and crossed the Atlantic Ocean, arriving safely in Liverpool, England, on June 12th 1917. On September 7th, Arthur Clifford started service, as an officer in the Royal Navy, a career he would enjoy for many years. He survived World War One, was promoted to sub-lieutenant on July 15th 1919, and again to Lieutenant two years later to the day in 1921. On November 22nd 1923, Arthur Clifford married Minetta Zara Eede in Portsmouth, England. His final promotion came on October 15th 1928, when he was promoted to Lieutenant Commander. With the start of World War Two, Lt/Cmdr Cresswell served on board the submarine depot ship H.M.S. Medway. It was during his service on this ship that, on September 1st 1941, while his ship was in Alexandria Egypt, he was mortally wounded during an enemy air attack. Lt/Cmdr Arthur Clifford Cresswell was buried in Plot 2, Row C, Grave 20, Alexandria (Hadra) War Memorial Cemetery, Egypt.

Service number: Lieut/Commander

Medals and Awards: British War Medal, Victory Medal (1914-1919), 1939-45 Star, Africa Star, War Medal 1939-45.

CRUISE, John Willis **Driver**
5th Brig., C.F.A. **WWI**

John Willis Cruise was born in Lachute, on April 13th 1899, son of John, a local farmer and Janet Ellen Bennett. He remained in Lachute until the 5th of June 1917, when he enlisted with the 79th Battery, Canadian Field Artillery. By then, Canada was in its third year of the War with no end in sight. He remained in Canada until November 19th 1917, when he boarded the troopship H.M.T. Megantic in Montreal and arrived in Liverpool, England on December 7th. On his arrival, he was assigned to the Reserve Brigade, Canadian Field Artillery in Witley, England until May 22nd 1918, when he crossed into France and proceeded to the Canadian Corps Reinforcement Camp in Aubin St-Vaast. On August 12th, he was posted to the 5th Brigade, Canadian Field Artillery. On August 27th, Driver Cruise's Brigade was supporting an attack by the Canadian Corps. While his battery was advancing to take up a new position in the rear of Cherisy, he received a gunshot wound to his left leg and was sent to the 8th Stationary Hospital in Wimereux, France. Sadly, John Willis Cruise succumbed to his wounds on September 4th. He was buried in Plot III, Row B, Grave 8 in the Terlincthun British Cemetery, Wimille, Pas-de-Calais, France.

Service number: 2522321

Medals and Awards: British War Medal and Victory Medal (1914-1919)

CRUISE, Lloyd J. **Private**
R.H.R. **WWII**

Lloyd Jackson Cruise was born on October 19th 1910, in Lachute, son of John and Janet Ellen

Bennett. He grew up and attended school in Lachute. On October 11th 1941, he married Grace Lavis also of Lachute. On November 23rd 1942, Lloyd enlisted in the Canadian Army in Montreal. At the time of his enlistment he reported being a truck driver and residing at 32 Brownsburg Road, Lachute with his wife. Immediately upon enlistment, he was assigned to No.4 District Depot in Montreal South. On December 3rd, he was assigned to No.41 Canadian Army Basic Training Centre in Huntingdon, Quebec. He spent several months in and out of this Training Centre, having attended the Canadian Machinegun Training and the Officer Training Centres in Trois-Rivières, Quebec. He remained in Canada until December 26th 1943, when he boarded a troopship and crossed the Atlantic. He arrived safely in the United Kingdom on January 4th 1944, and was assigned to No.5 Canadian Infantry Reinforcement Unit, Tourney Barracks, Aldershot, England. On March 14th, Pte Cruise was posted to a combat unit: The famed Black Watch Regiment. On July 6th, he crossed into mainland Europe and joined the 1st Battalion, The Black Watch (Royal Highland Regiment) of Canada. His older brother, Edgar James had also enlisted in the Canadian Army and by July 1944 was a prisoner of war in Germany. Edgar James survived the War. On July 25th 1944, the Royal Highlanders of Canada took part in a disastrous attack at May-Sur-Orne, France. It was during this attack that Pte Lloyd Jackson Cruise was killed in action. He was buried in Saint-Martin-de-Fontenay, France on August 13th. He was later exhumed and reburied in Plot IV, Row D, Grave 9 Bretteville-sur-Laize Canadian War Cemetery, Calvados, France.

Service number: D137945

Medals and Awards: 1939-45 Star, France and Germany Star, Defence Medal, the Canadian Volunteer Service Medal and clasp and the War Medal 1939-45.

CUNNINGHAM, Austin **Private**
73rd Bn **WWI**

Short history 73rd Battalion

Robert Austin Cunningham was born in Godmanchester Township, Huntingdon, Quebec on December 14th 1893, son of Alexander S., a farmer, and Isabella Burrows Ferns. Austin was a plasterer by trade. His father had been involved in the local politics of Godmanchester, having served on the council and as mayor. Alexander Cunningham died in 1912. Austin`s sister, Jennie Mary, married David John Rodger in 1916, a resident of St-Jerusalem parish, in Lachute. On September 15th 1915, Robert Austin enlisted in Montreal with the 73rd Battalion, Canadian Expeditionary Force and was posted to "D" Company, No.13 Platoon. He remained in Canada until he boarded the troopship R.M.S. Adriatic on March 31st 1916. This ship transported him to England where he landed in Liverpool on April 9th. He remained in England until August 13th, when he landed in Le Havre, France where he reached the Western Front. On March 1st 1917, the 73rd Battalion was part of a failed attack in which the Canadian Corps would employ gas in order to dislodge the defending Germans at Vimy Ridge. This attack was a total failure and the units involved suffered high casualties. On the 2nd, Austin Cunningham suffered a gunshot wound to the chest. He died as a result of his wounds at the Liverpool Merchants Hospital Etaples, France on March 21st. He was buried in Plot XXII, Row B, Grave 1 in the Etaples Military Cemetery, Pas-de-Calais, France.

Service number: 132506

Medals and Awards: British War Medal and Victory Medal (1914-1919)

DAVIS, Wesley T. **Private**
P.P.C.L.I. **WWII**

Wesley Thomas Davis was born in Arundel, Harrington Township on September 22nd 1919, son of William Thomas, a farmer and Sarah Thompson. He attended public school for six years, leaving at the age of 14. Wesley remained in Arundel all his young life. From 1934 to 1942 he was employed as a farm hand on his parents' farm in Arundel. His father William died in 1940. On December 4th 1941, he enrolled with the Canadian Army under the authority of the National Resources Mobilization Act of 1940 and was sent to No.41 Basic Training Centre in Huntingdon, Quebec. He remained in Huntingdon until he was sent to No.A-12 Advanced Training Centre in Farnham, Quebec, on February 5th 1942. On April 9th, he was transferred to "D" Company, Royal Rifles of Canada in Quebec. By June 27th, the R.R. of C. had been sent to Nanaimo, British Columbia and Rifleman Davis found himself away from Quebec for the first time. On October 30th, Rfmn Davis attested into the Active Formations of the Canadian Army while in New-Westminster, British Columbia. He remained with the R.R. of C. until December 29th, when he was sent to No.5 District Depot in Quebec. He left Canada on February 4th 1943, and arrived safely in the United Kingdom on the

13th. The next day he was sent to No.5 Canadian Infantry Reinforcement Unit at Tourney Barracks, Aldershot, England for extensive training. On May 12th, he was transferred to the Princess Patricia's Canadian Light Infantry and left the United Kingdom on June 29th, arriving in Italy on July 11th. On October 20th 1944, Pte Wesley Thomas Davis was killed during the P.P.C.L.I.'s attack across the Savio River in Italy. He was temporarily buried on the 23rd, in Grave 3, Row 4, 2nd Canadian Infantry Brigade cemetery in Cesena, Italy. He was later exhumed and reburied in Plot III, Row E, Grave 16, Cesena War Cemetery, Italy.

Service number: D157580

Medals and Awards: 1939-45 Star, Italy Star, the Canadian Volunteer Service Medal and clasp and the War Medal 1939-45.

DAWSON, Edward A. **W.O. II**
R.C.A.F. **WWII**

Edward Alexander Dawson was born in Grenville on May 4th 1919, son of Harris, a farmer, and Maude Hope. The family didn't remain in Grenville and moved to Iroquois Falls, Ontario, where Edward Alexander attended public school in Ansonville. He then attended the Iroquois Falls High School for four years. In 1937, he began employment with the Abitibi Power and Paper Company of Iroquois Falls, as a chemical assistant and as a paper maker. On October 9th 1940, Edward Alexander enrolled with the Algonquin Regiment and remained with this unit until he enlisted in the Royal Canadian Air Force on January 9th 1941, in North Bay, Ontario. The next day he was taken on strength with No.1 Manning Depot in Toronto. He then spent some time in Picton and Trenton, Ontario, being eventually assigned to No.1 Initial Training School also in Toronto. His pilot training was starting. On June 7th, he was sent to No.19 Elemental Flying Training School in Virden, Manitoba and remained until August 9th, when he was sent to No.12 Service Flying Training School in Brandon, also in Manitoba. Edward Alexander graduated and was awarded a pilot's flying badge on October 25th. On November 20th, he left Canada, arriving safely in the United Kingdom on December 7th, where he was sent to No.3 Personnel Reception Centre in Bournemouth, England. Edward Alexander remained in England for some time, being assigned to training units. On May 26th 1942, he was assigned to an operational unit, No.411 Squadron at R.A.F. Digby, England, flying Spitfire fighter aircrafts. On September 3rd, he was posted to No.253 Squadron in Hibaldstow, England, this time flying Hurricanes. On November 13th, the Squadron was transferred to RAF Maison Blanche, Algeria. On February 26th 1943, at about 1130hrs, while returning from a patrol, flying Hurricane HV904, about 2 to 3 miles from the coast, his engine cut out. F/Sgt Dawson radioed his intention to bail out and was seen exiting his aircraft. Sadly, his parachute became entangled with the aircraft's tail and he was instantly killed. His wingman, Sgt Kerville, orbited the wreckage until a rescue crew arrived on scene and retrieved F/Sgt Dawson's body. He was buried the next day with full military honours in the Philippeville cemetery. He was later exhumed and reburied in Plot VIII, Row F, Grave 6, Bone War Cemetery, Annaba, Algeria.

Service number: R69417

Medals and Awards: 1939-45 Star, Air Crew Europe Star, Africa Star, Defence Medal, the

Canadian Volunteer Service Medal and clasp and the War Medal 1939-45.

DEWAR, Frederick A. **Sapper**
R.C.E. **WWII**

Frederick Adam Dewar was born in Grenville Township on April 25th 1913, son of Adam, a farmer, and Ellen Grundy. Frederick resided in Grenville Township and attended school until the age of 14. In 1932, he began employment as a miner with the Canadian Refractories Company in Kilmar, Quebec and remained with this company until his enlistment with the Canadian Army. He married Ann Margaret Jowett on October 3rd 1936, in Grenville. Frederick enlisted with the Canadian Army on July 11th 1941, in Ottawa, Ontario. On August 31st, he was sent to No.31 Basic Training Centre in Cornwall, Ontario. He remained in Cornwall until October 1st, when he was sent to No.A5 Royal Canadian Engineers Training Centre in Petawawa, Ontario. Once his training completed, he was sent to Halifax where, on February 26th 1942, he boarded a troopship and sailed for Scotland, arriving safely and disembarking at Gourock on March 10th. Sapper Dewar was immediately taken on strength with No.1 Engineers Reinforcement Unit until June 26th, when he was transferred to No.8 Canadian Field Squadron. He was once again transferred, this time to No.1 Mechanical Equipment Company, Royal Canadian Engineers on April 5th 1943. On December 23rd 1943, while fixing wiring in the new mess hall for his unit, Sapper Frederick Adam Dewar suffered an electric shock. He died at 1212hrs. He was buried in Plot 47, Row J, Grave 4, Brookwood Military Cemetery, Surrey, United Kingdom.

Service number: C2769

Medals and Awards: Defence Medal, the Canadian Volunteer Service Medal and clasp and the War Medal 1939-45.

DEWAR, James A. **Private**
46th Bn **WWI**

James Alexander Dewar was born on April 10th 1887, in Lost River, son of William and Catherine Ferguson. William was a farmer and the family was residing on the 6th concession of Wentworth Township. Like his father, James Alexander was a farmer. On June 2nd 1916, he enlisted with the 229th Overseas Battalion in Rouleau, Saskatchewan, the first of two brothers to enlist, the other being Willie who also enlisted in Rouleau in the same Battalion but a few months later. He remained in Canada until his Battalion boarded the troopship S.S. Northland in Halifax, Nova Scotia on April 17th 1917, reaching England safely on the 29th. Once in England, he proceeded to Bramshott where, he transferred to the 19th Reserve Battalion and, once again, to the 46th Battalion on September 10th. He arrived in France and the Western Front a few days later. In October 1917, the 46th Battalion was taking part in the offensive at Passchendaele. James Alexander was seriously wounded on the 27th during this battle, having suffered a gunshot wound to his left leg and face. Private Dewar succumbed to his injuries on November 23rd 1917, at No.9 General Hospital in Rouen, France. He had been on the Front a little over one month. He was buried in Plot III, Grave 12B in the St-Sever Cemetery Extension, Rouen, France.

Service number: 1010112

Medals and Awards: British War Medal and Victory Medal (1914-1919)

DE WITT, William N. **F/Officer**
R.C.A.F. **WWII**

LAC/BAC

William Norton Dewitt was born in Outremont, Quebec on March 19th 1924, son of Jacob, a lawyer, and Julia Maria Hill. This family resided in St-Andrews East. William was educated in St-Andrews East, having attended schools from 1930 to 1940, and then spent two years at West Hill High School in Montreal, leaving in 1942. He was then employed by the Canadian National Railways, in Montreal, as a timekeeper and clerk. On March 31st 1943, he enlisted with the Royal Canadian Air Force in Montreal and was taken on strength with No.5 Manning Depot in Lachine, Quebec. Three of his brothers had already enlisted and were serving overseas. All three survived the War. On May 18th, William was sent to No.8 Service Flying Training School in Moncton, New Brunswick. On June 13th, he was sent to No.1 Initial Training School in Toronto, Ontario until September 10th, when he was sent to No.2 Bombing and Gunnery School in Mossbank, Saskatchewan. From there, he proceeded to No.2 Air Observer School in Edmonton, Alberta on January 2nd, 1944. On April 10th, he boarded a troopship in Halifax and crossed the Atlantic, landing safely in the United Kingdom on the 18th. He was assigned to No.3 Personnel Reception Centre, in Bournemouth, England. From No.3, he was sent to No.2 Advanced Flying Unit, No.24 Operational Training Unit and finally posted to a Canadian Bomber Squadron, the 419th, in Middleton St.George, England on February 12th 1945. On March 6th 1945, No.419 Squadron was detailed to take part in a massive 760 aircraft raid on Chemnitz, Germany. The aircrafts encountered problems from the start as some of them crashed after take-off due to icy conditions. At 0130hrs, on its return leg, the Lancaster Mark X number KB.845 bomber in which F/O De Witt was a crew member crashed, at Drayton Parsloe, England. The aircraft may have been hit by enemy canon shells or crashed due to severe icing. There were no survivors. F/O William Norton De Witt was buried in Plot 50, Row E, Grave 6, Brookwood Military Cemetery, Surrey, England.

Service number: J41610

Medals and Awards: 1939-45 Star, France and Germany Star, Defence Medal, the Canadian Volunteer Service Medal and clasp and the War Medal 1939-45.

DICKINSON, John H. **Private**
3rd Bn **WWI**

John Henry Dickinson was born in St-Peters Parish, Brighton, Sussex, England, on February 9th 1893, son of John Henry, a blacksmith's striker and Alice Maud Woolgar. John immigrated to Canada with his mother and siblings in 1908, having left Liverpool, England on October 8th, and arriving in Quebec on the 19th. On October 7th 1914, John enlisted with "A" Company, 23rd Provisional Battalion, Canadian Expeditionary Force in Montreal. He reported being a waiter and his mother, Alice, residing in Rockway Valley, Papineau, Quebec. He remained in Canada until February 23rd 1915, when he boarded the troopship S.S. Missanabie and left for the War, arriving safely in England. On May 3rd, he was transferred to the 3rd Battalion in France. Pte Dickinson became ill in June while in the vicinity of Festubert. He was evacuated out of the Front lines and sent back to England where he was diagnosed with pulmonary tuberculosis. His condition worsened. The following October, he was repatriated to Canada, being no longer medically fit for service. He was discharged from the Canadian Army on April 15th 1916. On April 26th, John Henry was married to Elsie Warham in Montreal. John never recuperated from his tuberculosis and, on August 6th 1917, he died. At the time of his death, he was residing in Arundel. He was buried in the Amherst (St. George's) Anglican Church Cemetery, Quebec.

Service number: 63308

Medals and Awards: 1914-1915 Star, British War Medal and Victory Medal (1914-1919)

DIXON, George **Private**
14th Bn **WWI**

George Dixon was born on November 8th 1893, in Liverpool, England. He later immigrated to Canada. During his years in Canada prior to the War, he served a few weeks with the 17th Hussars. He was a friend of Mr William J. Elliott of Lachute. On September 15th 1915, he enlisted with "D" Company of the 73rd Battalion and was re-assigned to the 148th Overseas Battalion prior to leaving for England. On September 26th 1916, he sailed for England on board the troopship S.S. Laconia and disembarked in Liverpool on October 6th. He remained in England until December 13th, when he was transferred to the 14th Battalion and arrived with his new unit and on the Western Front in France the next day. On February 12th 1917, he was temporarily attached to the 2nd Canadian Tunneling Company. A few days later, he was admitted to the 15th Casualty Clearing

Station suffering from a swollen foot. He was returned to the 14th Battalion on March 20th 1917. On April 9th, the day the Canadian Corps attacked Vimy Ridge, Pte George Dixon was killed in action during this historical attack. He was buried in Plot I, Row A Grave 17 in the Nine Elms Military Cemetery, Thelus, Pas-de-Calais, France.

Service number: 132489

Medals and Awards: British War Medal and Victory Medal (1914-1919)

DOIG, Howard L. **Trooper**
3rd C.A.C.R.U. **WWII**

Howard Lawrence Doig was born in Lachute on October 29th 1919, son of Robert and Eva Doig. He attended school and later worked at the Defence Industries Ltd in Brownsburg as a tool setter. Howard Lawrence enlisted in the Canadian Army on May 3rd 1941 in Montreal. At that time he stated residing at 5502 Isabella Avenue, Montreal, being a driver and mechanic by trade and having served at No.41 Militia Training Centre in Huntingdon, Quebec since March 1941. Upon enlistment, he was assigned to No.4 District Depot in Montreal South. On June 26th, he was transferred to the 1st Canadian Armored Division in Borden, Ontario. On the 16th of July, he was assigned to HQ Squadron, 6th Hussars. On August 18th, he proceeded to No.20 Basic Training Centre in Brantford, Ontario. He remained in Canada until he left for the United Kingdom on November 14th, and arrived in Liverpool, England on the 24th. On May 1st 1942, he was assigned to the 3rd Canadian Armoured Corps Reinforcement Unit. On July 24th, Trooper Doig became ill and was admitted to the Royal Victoria Hospital, Netley Hound, Southampton, England. On August

27th 1942, Trooper Doig died of streptococcal septicaemia. He was buried in Plot 38, Row H, Grave 3, Brookwood Cemetery, Surrey, United Kingdom.

Service number: D92

Medals and Awards: Defence Medal, the Canadian Volunteer Service Medal and clasp and the War Medal 1939-45.

DORION, Lester L. **Private**
Perth Regt. **WWII**

Lester Lomax Dorion was born in Montreal on October 16th 1915, son of Albert Leister, a farmer residing in St-Andrews East, and Ann Lomax. His mother died in 1917. Lester attended school until the age of 15, after two years of High School. He resided in St-Andrews East all his young life. He worked as a stone driller for Ayers Woolen Mill Company of Lachute from 1934 to 1936 and was employed by F.W. Boissevain as a chauffeur from 1936 to 1940. On July 30th 1940, Lester enlisted in the Canadian Army in Montreal and was immediately taken on strength with the Victoria Rifles of Canada. His enlistment allowed him to travel throughout Canada from coast to coast. He remained in Canada until March 27th 1943, when he left Canada and crossed the Atlantic Ocean for the United Kingdom, arriving on April 4th. He was taken on strength with No.3 Canadian Infantry Reinforcement Unit the next day and transferred to the Perth Regiment on June 18th. He remained in the U.K. until October 26th, when he embarked for the Mediterranean Theatre of Operations disembarking in Italy on November 8th. The Italian Campaign proved to be difficult for the Canadian troops and the Perth Regiment was involved in combat in often difficult conditions and terrain. On May 26th 1944, Pte Lester Lomax Dorion was killed in action during the difficult fighting around Cassino, Italy and was buried the next day. He was later exhumed and carefully reburied in Plot V, Row F, Grave 5, Cassino War Cemetery, Italy.

Service number: D71247

Medals and Awards: 1939-45 Star, Italy Star, Defence Medal, the Canadian Volunteer Service Medal and clasp and the War Medal 1939-45.

DOUGLAS, Roland K. R.F.C. — 2nd Lieutenant WWI

St . Mungo's Centennial

Roland Keith Douglas was born on June 7th 1898, son of John and Georgina Noyes, farmers of Chatham Township. He was a student at the Lachute Academy from 1912 to 1914. He joined the Royal Flying Corps on February 17th 1918, as a 2/Lt. He was posted to No.81 Squadron on March 23rd. On August 11th 1918, he took off from his base at Savy, France flying an offensive patrol mission with his Sopwith Dolphin number C4043 fighter aircraft. He had been observed in combat with enemy aircrafts east of Albert and failed to return to his base. It was later reported he had been captured and was a prisoner of war and held at the Meschede POW Camp in Germany and had been wounded. 2/Lt Douglas did not survive his injuries as he died while still in a prisoner of war camp on November 26th 1918, 17 days after the Armistice. He had been interred in the British part, Grave 45, Meschede POW cemetery. He was later exhumed and re-interred in Plot V, Row F, Grave 2, Niederzwehren Cemetery, Hessen, Germany.

Service number: 2/Lt

Medals and Awards: British War Medal and Victory Medal (1914-1919)

DREW, Charles C. **F/Officer**
R.C.A.F. **WWII**

LAC/BAC

Charles Cyril Drew was born on April 1st 1917, in Lachute, son of John H., a medical doctor and Ruth Rae Walker. Charles attended the Lachute Academy then proceeded to the Lachute High School and graduated in 1935. His mother and father passed away in 1936 and 1938 respectively. Charles had started working for Bell Telephone Company of Canada on May 5th 1936, being assigned to various duties of the Construction Department, and moved up to the position of foreman. He had a fondness for radios having built radio receivers and operated amateur radio phone transmitters. Charles was also involved in numerous sports like hockey, swimming, tennis, badminton and baseball. Two of his brothers, John Sydney and William Winston McOuat also served in the R.C.A.F. and survived the War. Charles enlisted in the Royal Canadian Air Force on September 14th 1940, in Montreal. He was immediately assigned to No.1 Manning Depot in Toronto, Ontario. On October 8th, he proceeded to Eastern Air Command in Sydney, Nova Scotia. On February 20th 1941, he was sent to No.4 Elemental Flying Training School in Windsor Mills, Quebec. His training continued. On April 10th, he was sent to No.9 Service Flying Training School in Summerside, P.E.I. and again sent to No.2 Service Flying Training School in Uplands, Ontario on September 25th. During his training, he rose through the ranks, was promoted to Warrant Officer II and qualified on the Finch, Harvard and Hanson aircrafts. WOII Drew became a flying instructor. He was commissioned a Pilot Officer on October 13th 1942. His work was exemplary and as a result, on April 16th 1943, he was awarded the Air Force Cross. The recommendation set forth by his superiors read as follows:

> *"This Warrant Officer has been employed as a flying instructor at #2 S.F.T.S. for the past 15 months. He has worked exceedingly hard with the sole object in mind of turning out pilots of a high standard. The example he has set by his deportment, initiative and devotion to duty as an instructor is especially commendable. Many skillful pilots have been trained by this efficient and painstaking Warrant Officer during the more than 1400 hours service flying that he now has to his credit as a flying instructor."*

On January 22nd 1943, he returned to Summerside, having been posted to No.1 General Reconnaissance Squadron. He remained in Canada until he boarded a troopship and left Canada on May 9th, and arrived safely in the United Kingdom on the 23rd. He was assigned to a couple of transit units until December 14th, when he was posted to No.540 Squadron, R.A.F Leuchars, Scotland, a long range reconnaissance unit, flying Mosquito aircrafts. On April 13th

1944, at about 0950hrs, F/O Drew took off from R.A.F. Station Benson, England, in Mosquito MkIX LR.416 on a photographic reconnaissance mission in the area of Munich, Germany. At about 1040hrs, the aircraft sent a return signal. For an unknown reason, on the return flight, the Mosquito crashed one and a half miles west of Kingston-Bagpuize, England. Observers reported seeing the aircraft breaking cloud cover in a steep dive and at about one thousand feet breaking apart. Charles Cyril Drew and the navigator, Sgt J.I. Shaer were instantly killed. F/O Drew was buried in plot 48, Row F, Grave 6, Brookwood Military Cemetery, Surrey, United Kingdom.

Service number: J23033

Medals and Awards: Air Force Cross, 1939-45 Star, Atlantic Star, Defence Medal, the Canadian Volunteer Service Medal and clasp and the War Medal 1939-45.

DRINKWATER, Charles **Private**
21st Bn **WWI**

Charles Drinkwater was born on September 12th 1887, in London England, son of Alfred, a cab driver, and Mary Ann Rush. He immigrated to Canada with his wife, Mary and two children, and reported going to Lachute to work as a farm labourer. For an unknown reason, he enlisted in the Canadian Expeditionary Force on October 30th 1914, in Montreal, using the name of John Sullivan. He enlisted with the Canadian Army Veterinary Corps and went overseas to England sometime before the 1st of May 1915. On this date, he proceeded to Continental Europe and joined the 1st Canadian Veterinary Hospital in Rouen, France. Charles appears to have been quite a character. On October 12th 1915, he was sentenced to 14 days C.B. for being drunk on active duty. Again in 1916 he found himself in trouble. On February 23rd 1916, he was confined while awaiting his trial for disobeying a lawful order. On the 28th, he was tried and found guilty by Field General Court Martial and was sentenced to 56 days of Field Punishment Number 1. When released, he was assigned to several units before finally reaching the ranks of the 21st Battalion on the 3rd of November 1916. Between the 15th and 17th of August 1918, Pte Drinkwater was wounded while participating in an attack in the area of Lens, France. He died on the 17th. Charles Drinkwater was buried in plot I, Row K, Grave 4, Aix-Noulette Cummunal Cemetery Extension, Pas-de-Calais, France.

Service number: 48510

Medals and Awards: 1914-1915 Star, British War Medal and Victory Medal (1914-1919)

DUBEAU, Bentley B. **Trooper**
R.C.A.C. **WWII**

Bentley Boyd Dubeau was born in Arundel on July 16th 1925, son of Arthur and Florence Samson. He attended public school for six years, leaving at the age of 16. Two of Bentley's brothers, namely John Arthur and Alfred Sydney had enlisted in the Canadian Forces and had been sent Overseas. Both survived the War. In 1942, he became employed for Mr McGibbon out of Morin Heights, a road contractor, as a laborer. On March 20th 1944, Bentley enlisted in the Canadian Armoured Corps in Montreal and was sent to No.23 Basic Training Centre in Newmarket, Ontario. He remained at this training center until March 1945. Tragically, on March 29th 1945, at about 1920hrs,

Trooper Bentley Boyd Dubeau was a passenger in a motor vehicle when it collided with a C.N.R. train in Newmarket. Bentley and the driver did not survive the accident. A Court of Inquiry returned a verdict of no blame assigned to the driver. On April 2nd, he was buried in Plot 14, Section A, Arundel (Methodist) cemetery.

Service number: D144630

Medals and Awards: The Canadian Volunteer Service Medal and the War Medal 1939-45.

DUDLEY, Griffith **Private**
24th Bn **WWI**

Griffith Ernest Rollins Dudley was born in Granby, Quebec on August 6th 1896, son of Ernest Eugene and Elizabeth Catherine Roberts. His childhood is a mystery. Griffith and his brother Eugene enlisted with the 148th Overseas Battalion, C.E.F. on July 3rd 1916. Eugene would survive the War and by 1920 was residing in St-Andrews. At the time of his enlistment, Griffith was residing in Montreal and was a fruit grower. His mother, Elizabeth, had remarried and was residing in Florida. Griffith had served in the Canadian Militia, having seen service with the 55th Irish Canadian Rangers. He remained in Canada until September 27th 1916, when he boarded the troopship S.S. Laconia. He reached the shores of England safely, landing in Liverpool on October 6th. He proceeded to Witley Camp and remained there until December 17th, when he crossed into Mainland Europe and joined his new unit, the 24th Battalion. On April 9th 1917, the Canadian Corps assaulted Vimy Ridge. The 24th Battalion was part of this historic attack. It was during this attack that Pte Griffith Dudley was hit by shrapnel to his back. He was evacuated out of the lines and sent to No.32 Stationary Hospital, where, on April 12th, he died. He was buried in Plot II, Row G, Grave 4, Wimereux Communal Cemetery, Pas-de-Calais, France.

Service number: 919696

Medals and Awards: British War Medal and Victory Medal (1914-1919)

DUMAS, Arthur **Private**
13th Bn **WWI**

Joseph Arthur Dumas was born in Montreal on July 21st 1879, son of Napoléon and Philomène Huard. He remained in Montreal, but by 1891, this family had moved to Lachute. On November 18th 1902, Arthur married Clémentine Thibeau in Lachute. On March 7th 1917, he enlisted in the Canadian Expeditionary Force with the 2nd Reinforcement Draft, 5th Royal Highlanders of Canada. Arthur had prior military service, having served with the 11th Battalion and the 5th Royal Highlanders of Canada. Further, he had worked as a barber. He arrived in England on April 22nd, having crossed on the S.S. Canada. On his arrival, he was transferred to the 20th Reserve Battalion and remained with this Battalion until November 17th 1917, when Arthur proceeded to France and was posted to the 13th Battalion. He remained in France with the Battalion until April 6th 1918, when he was severely wounded while in the trenches. He died the same day at No.8 Casualty Clearing Station. He was buried in Plot VI, Row F, Grave 46 in the Duisans British Cemetery, Etrun, Pas-de-Calais, France.
Service number: 2075384

Medals and Awards: British War Medal and Victory Medal (1914-1919)

FISH, James G. **Sergeant**
R.H.R. **WWII**

James Garth Fish was born in Montreal, Quebec on September 11th 1911, son of James Alexander and Edith Isabelle Williams. He attended school and left after two years of High School. In 1932, he began employment with the Dominion Textile Company Ltd at Victoria Square in Montreal, as an office clerk. He remained at their employ until his enlistment into the Canadian Army. Garth enlisted with the 17th Duke of York Royal Canadian Hussars, a militia unit in Montreal, on July 8th 1940. He reported that he had served for two years with Cadets, was residing at 83 Ballantyne Avenue in Montreal and his father was residing in Dunany near Lachute. His younger brother, William Thomas, also enlisted with the Royal Canadian Air Force during the War. He survived the conflict. James Garth attended several training camps and remained with this unit until May 26th 1942, when he enlisted with the Canadian Army's 2nd Battalion, The Black Watch (Royal Highland Regiment) of Canada. On May 29th, he joined the Battalion in Westmount Barracks and was appointed an acting/sergeant. On January 4th 1943, his promotion to sergeant was confirmed. He remained in Canada until June 11th, when he boarded a troopship, and left Canada for the United Kingdom and the War. He landed safely on the 18th, and proceeded to No.5 Canadian Infantry Reinforcement Unit at Tourney Barracks, Aldershot, England for further training. He remained with this Unit until August 6th, when he joined The Black Watch (Royal Highland Regiment) of Canada. Sgt Fish left the United Kingdom and landed in France on July 6th 1944. On July 25th 1944, the Royal Highlanders of Canada took part in a disastrous attack at May-Sur-Orne, France. It was during this attack that Sgt James Garth Fish was killed in action. He was temporarily buried in the Saint-Martin-de-Fontenay cemetery on August 14th. He was later exhumed and re-burried in Plot I, Row E, Grave 8, Bretteville-Sur-Laize Canadian War Cemetery, Calvados, France.

Service number: D86220

Medals and Awards: 1939-45 Star, France and Germany Star, Defence Medal, the Canadian Volunteer Service Medal and clasp and the War Medal 1939-45.

FISHER, Norman **Private**
13th Bn **WWI**

Short history 73rd Battalion

Norman Fisher was born on June 12th 1896, in Brownsburg, son of George and Mary MacDonald. Norman was the half-brother of Alvin Charles Roberts who was killed in action in France in 1944. George was first generation Canadian, his parents being from England. Norman resided in Chatham Township until about 1906, when his father died in an industrial explosion while working at the Dominion Cartridge Company in Brownsburg. His mother, Mary, remarried the same year to Charles Roberts, also of Brownsburg. By 1911, Norman and his family found themselves residing in Gananoque, Ontario. On October 27th 1915, he enlisted with the Canadian Expeditionary Force and joined the 73rd Battalion in Montreal. At the time of his enlistment, his mother was residing on St-James Street in Montreal and he was a quarryman by trade. He remained in Canada until

March 31st 1916, when he left Halifax on board the troopship S.S. Adriatic bound for England. He arrived on April 10th, where he transferred to the 13th Battalion on June 18th. He landed in France the next day and joined his Battalion in Flanders Fields also known as the Western Front. By then, the Great War was in its second year with no end in sight. Pte Norman Fisher was reported missing and wounded on September 4th 1916, following action in which his Battalion was heavily shelled and counter-attacked by German Forces in the vicinity of Courcelette, France. His body was never found and was listed on the Vimy Memorial until 1940, when his body was found about one mile south-west of Mouquet Farms. He was properly reburied in Plot IX, Row F, Grave 43 in the London Cemetery Extension, High Wood, Longueval, France.

Service number: 133048

Medals and Awards: British War Medal and Victory Medal (1914-1919)

FOX, Evan **L/Bombardier**
1st L.A.A. **WWII**

Evan Daniel Fox was born in Harrington on July 24th 1917, son of Dougal and Elizabeth Catherine Smith. His education is unknown. Evan spent his life residing with his parents in Grenville Township and was employed as a miner with the Canadian Refractories Ltd. On July 29th 1940, he enlisted with the Canadian Army in Westmount, Quebec and was taken on strength with No.2 Company, Canadian Forestry Corps. He remained in Canada until he boarded a troopship in Halifax on February 15th 1941, arriving safely in the United Kingdom and disembarking in Gourock, Scotland on March 1st. He was sent to Ballogie,

Scotland with No.2 Company. On the 10th, No.2 Company was sent to Blair Atholl, also in Scotland, and Pte Fox followed. He remained in Scotland with this Company until August 9th 1943, when he was transferred to No.3 Canadian Artillery Reinforcement Unit. He remained in the United Kingdom until October 27th, when he boarded a troopship and sailed for the Mediterranean Theater of War, arriving in Italy on November 9th. He was transferred to No.1 Light Anti-Aircraft Battalion on March 1st 1944, in Lanciano, Italy and was promoted to Lance Bombardier on August 24th. On September 2nd 1944, L/Bmdr Evan Fox was killed in action while the 1st was involved in combat against German forces in the area of Tomba Di Pesaro. He was temporarily buried in Row B, Grave 1, near the Di Pesaro Cemetery and later exhumed and reburied on May 7th 1945, in Plot I, Row H, Grave 3, Gradara War Cemetery, Italy.

Service number: D110160

Medals and Awards: 1939-45 Star, Italy Star, Defence Medal, the Canadian Volunteer Service Medal and clasp and the War Medal 1939-45.

GALL, Hugh W. **Lieutenant**
R.H.R. **WWII**

H. W. Gall, B.A.
Photo courtesy of Bishop's University Archives, Sherbrooke

Hugh Wilson Gall was born in Lachute on July 28th 1913, son of Hugh Mossman, a merchant and Flora Mabel Wilson. Hugh grew up in Lachute, attended school and graduated from the Lachute High School in 1931. He then continued his education, attending Bishop's University in Lennoxville,

Quebec and graduated in 1934 obtaining his B.A. In 1935 he obtained his Teacher's Diploma and became a teacher in Westmount, Quebec. Hugh married Olivia Margaret Scoggie in Montreal on March 23rd 1940. Hugh was commissioned as a 2nd Lieutenant while in McGill's Canadian Officers Training Corps. On September 12th 1940, he was assigned to No.4 District Depot. On the 28th, he was sent to No.43 Training Centre in Sherbrooke, Quebec until February 17th 1941, when he was transferred to No.41 Training Centre in Huntingdon, Quebec. On September 14th, he attested into the Canadian Army Regular Force and remained in Huntingdon for further training. On June 6th 1942, he was transferred to the 2nd Battalion, The Black Watch (Royal Highland Regiment) of Canada and assigned to Westmount Barracks in Montreal. On July 26th, he was once again transferred. This time he was sent to Camp Sussex, New Brunswick. His training continued transferring to Halifax Nova Scotia, Woodstock Ontario, Debert Nova Scotia, Montreal and Farnham Quebec. Lieut. Gall left Canada, boarding a troopship and crossing the Atlantic on December 26th 1943, and arrived safely on January 3rd 1944. Once in England, over the course of several months, he was assigned to No.5 and then to No.4 Canadian Infantry Reinforcement Units for further training. On August 13th 1944, Lieut. Gall landed in France and joined the 1st Battalion, the Black Watch (Royal Highland Regiment) of Canada. His War was short lived. Eight days after arriving in France, Lieut. Hugh Wilson Gall was killed in the vicinity of Vimoutiers, when the Battalion ran into enemy opposition. He was buried initially by the Calvary cemetery in the Vimoutiers area. He was later exhumed and reburied in Plot XVIII, Row B, Grave 11 Bretteville-sur-Laize Canadian War Cemetery, Calvados, France.

Service number: Lieutenant

Medals and Awards: 1939-45 Star, France and Germany Star, Defence Medal, the Canadian Volunteer Service Medal and clasp and the War Medal 1939-45.

GALLERY, William Leo **Private**
6th C.M.G.C. **WWI**

William Leo Gallery was born in St-John, New-Brunswick on May 4th 1898, son of Patrick, a teamster and Francis Hammersley. By 1901 this family had moved to Brownsburg. Patrick Gallery died in 1912 and Frances re-married to John Reid also from Brownsburg in 1915. William Leo served with the 5th Royal Highlanders of Canada, a militia unit, until August 28th 1916, when he enlisted with the 5th R.H.C. Draft, Canadian Expeditionary Force. His brother, John Edwin, had enlisted a couple of months prior to him. John Edwin survived the War. By this time William Leo was residing in Quebec City. He remained in Canada until he boarded the troopship S.S. Olympic in Halifax on December 15th 1916. He landed safely in Liverpool, England on the 26th. On the 30th, he was assigned to the 92nd Battalion in East Sandling. For the next four months, he was transferred to different units until April 28th 1917, when he was transferred to the 6th Machine Gun Company and he joined this unit in the field the next day. He remained with the 6th until he was instantly killed by an enemy shell while on ration party in the vicinity of Passchendaele on November 11th 1917. Private William Leo Gallery was buried in Plot I, Row C, Grave 37 in the Tyne Cot Cemetery, West-Vlaanderen, Belgium.

Service number: 228882

Medals and Awards: British War Medal and Victory Medal (1914-1919)

GASTON, William **Private**
1st Bn **WWI**

St . Mungo's Centennial

William Allan Gaston was born on February 16th 1898, in Hawkesbury, Ontario, son of James and Lilly Simpson. His mother died prior to 1911 and William Allan found himself living with his father and mother's relatives in Hawkesbury. He enlisted with the 87th Battalion, The Canadian Grenadier Guards, on December 6th 1915, in Montreal and listed his trade as being a sailor. At this time he further listed his uncle, Hastings Nowlan from Carillon, as his next-of-kin. He left Canada for the War on board the troopship S.S. Empress of Britain on April 23rd 1916, and landed in England on the 5th of May. He was transferred to the 1st Battalion on June 18th joining his unit in France the next day. A mere three weeks later, on July 9th 1916, Pte William Gaston, along with several of his comrades, was buried by shell fire in the trenches in the vicinity of Maple Copse, Belgium. The 1st Battalion had suffered heavily from German guns, having lost 100 men killed and wounded on that day. His body was never found. He was 18 years old. He is commemorated on the Menin Gate Memorial in Ieper, West-Vlaanderen, Belgium.

Service number: 177980

Medals and Awards: British War Medal and Victory Medal (1914-1919)

GAUDREAULT, Robert A.J. Regt Chaudière | **Private WWII**

Robert Albany Joseph Gaudreault was born in Shawinigan Falls, Quebec, on November 4th 1921, son of Napoleon, a farmer, and Délima Naud. The family moved to the Abitibi area of Quebec. Robert attended public school at the La Tuque College until 1936. Between 1936 and 1941, he worked on and off as a lumberman for the Spruce Falls Lumber Company in Kapuskasing, Ontario. On November 23rd 1942, he enlisted in Toronto with the Canadian Army. At the time of his enlistment, he reported residing in Beaucanton, Quebec and being a farmer by trade. He was immediately taken on strength with No.2 District Depot in Toronto, Ontario. On December 5th, he was sent to No.26 Basic Training Centre in Orillia, Ontario until July 4th 1943, when he was reassigned to No.2 District Depot. Robert struggled with his training in Ontario, speaking no English whatsoever. He remained with this unit until August 25th, when he was assigned to No.5 District Depot in Lauzon, Quebec. He remained in Canada until he boarded a troopship and left Canada on May 1st 1944, arriving in the United Kingdom on the 7th. He was immediately taken on strength with No.6 Canadian Infantry Reinforcement Unit in Farnley Park, Otley, England. On June 8th, he crossed the English Channel for France and joined with his new unit, the Régiment de la Chaudière. Robert survived the rigors of combat and the War but it had a profound effect on his health. His service record indicates he suffered heavily from nervousness and at times his extremities would tremble. After the War he was repatriated to

Canada and on March 14th 1946, was discharged from the Canadian Army. Robert married Rose-Alma Bélanger in Montreal on December 2nd 1946. The couple moved to 35 Bedard in Lachute. On February 20th 1947, Pte Robert Albany Joseph Gaudreault died of a cerebral hemorrhage at the Queen Mary Veteran's Hospital in Montreal. The attending physician reported that the death was directly related to his military service. He was buried in Section M, Lot 3410, Grave 1023, Côte des Neiges cemetery, Montreal, Quebec.

Service number: B136536

Medals and Awards: 1939-45 Star, France and Germany Star, the Canadian Volunteer Service Medal and clasp and the War Medal 1939-45.

GELINAS, Roland **L/Corporal**
Régt. Maison. **WWII**

Joseph Rosario Roland Gélinas was born in Montreal on February 13th 1914, son of Cyprien, a typographer and Amanda Poirier. Roland grew up in Montreal, attending school until grade seven. On October 17th 1934, he married Liliane Roy in Montreal. By 1944, Roland's wife and children were residing in Carillon. In 1936, Roland began employment with Peel Windsor Garage in Montreal as a serviceman and remained at their employ until June 14th 1940, when he enlisted with the Canadian Army in Montreal. He was taken on strength the same day with the Régiment de Maisonneuve and remained in Canada only a few months. On August 24th, he boarded a troopship in Halifax, Nova Scotia and crossed the Atlantic, landing safely in Gourock, Scotland on September 5th. He remained in the United Kingdom, training with his

Regiment until July 8th 1944, when he arrived in France. On September 8th, he was promoted to Lance Corporal. On October 2nd 1944, L/Cpl Gélinas was killed instantly when the motorcycle he was riding failed to negotiate a sharp curve and collided with a tree in the vicinity of Gravenwezel, Belgium. A Court of Inquiry concluded that although the cause of the accident was unknown, that L/Cpl Gélinas could not be blamed. He was buried the same day in Row 1, Grave 9, Candonchlaerhoef Cemetery in Belgium. He was later exhumed and reburied in Plot VIII, Row E, Grave 7, Bergen-Op-Zoom Canadian War Cemetery, Noord-Brabant, Holland.

Service number: D57381

Medals and Awards: 1939-45 Star, France and Germany Star, Defence Medal, the Canadian Volunteer Service Medal and clasp and the War Medal 1939-45.

GIRARD, Leo **Private**
22nd Bn **WWI**

Leo (Leon) Girard was born in St-Andrews on April 21st 1882, the son of Pierre, a carpenter, and Marie Melina Boyer. He remained in Argenteuil for some years. In 1905, he married Corinne Payette in the St-Louis-de-France parish in Montreal. On August 17th 1917, he enlisted with the Quebec Reserve Depot, Canadian Expeditionary Force in Quebec City. At the time of his enlistment, he resided in Carillon and was an accountant by trade. On September 26th, he transferred to the 258th Battalion. He remained in Canada until he left for England on October 4th 1917, arriving in England on the 17th, and immediately transferred to the 10th Reserve Battalion in Witley. He remained with the 10th in

England until he crossed to mainland Europe and joined his new unit, the 22nd Battalion in France. On April 21st 1918, Leo came down with a case of dermatitis. It had to be quite severe as he remained in the military hospitals until May 20th, when he was released and sent to the Canadian Corps Reinforcement Camp. There, he remained, until he rejoined the 22nd Battalion on June 19th. On August 27th 1918, Pte Leo Girard was instantly killed by enemy machinegun fire while taking part, with the Battalion, in an attack and advance east of the Wancourt to Cherisy area near Arras. He was buried in Row C, Grave 36 in the Quebec Cemetery, Cherisy, Pas-de-Calais, France.

Service number: 1105256

Medals and Awards: British War Medal and Victory Medal (1914-1919)

GIROUX, Henri **Private**
R.C.A.S.C. **WWII**

Godefroi-Henri Giroux was born in St-Andrews on June 17th 1922, son of Felix, a farmer, and Olivine Legault. He spent his early life in Chatham Township helping on his parents' farm. He left school at age 11 having attended for four years. Henri enlisted with the Canadian Army on June 16th 1941, in Montreal and was immediately taken on strength with No.4 District Depot. On July 22nd, he was sent to his unit, No.1 Bridge Company, Royal Canadian Army Service Corps in Mt-Bruno, Quebec. He remained in Mt-Bruno until he proceeded to Halifax, Nova Scotia and boarded a troopship on November 13th, bound for England. He arrived safely and landed in Liverpool on the 23rd. In 1942, he was assigned to No.85 Bridge Company in Cobham, England.

He remained in the United Kingdom until July 7th 1944, when he landed in France. On September 14th 1944, Pte Henri Giroux was killed while operating a vehicle during operations with the British 44th Brigade in Belgium. The truck he was driving was hit by enemy mortar shell. On October 29th, he was temporarily buried in the St-Dymphe churchyard in Geel, Belgium. He was later exhumed and reburied in Plot I, Row B, Grave 16, Geel War Cemetery, Antwerpen, Belgium.

Service number: D123335

Medals and Awards: 1939-45 Star, France and Germany Star, Defence Medal, the Canadian Volunteer Service Medal and clasp and the War Medal 1939-45.

GLEADALL, George **Lieutenant**
R.C.A. **WWII**

George Gleadall was born in Sheffield, Yorkshire, England on February 6th 1915, son of A. and Rose Gleadall. George attended Carfield School in Sheffield, until 1929. On July 4th 1929, George boarded the ship S.S. Duchess of York in Liverpool and left England to immigrate to Canada, arriving in Quebec on the 12th. Once in Quebec, he travelled to the British Immigration and Colonization Association hostel in Montreal with the intention to work on a farm. By 1935, George was residing in St-Jerusalem parish in Lachute. From 1937 to 1939, he worked at the Dr. G.R. McCall farm in Lachute as a manager. During the same years, he was a student of agriculture at MacDonald's College in Montreal and obtained a diploma in 1940. During his years at MacDonald's he was enrolled with the Canadian Officer Training Corps at McGill

University. On April 3rd 1940, George enlisted with the Canadian Army in Montreal and was immediately taken on strength with the 1st Survey Regiment & Battery, Royal Canadian Artillery. He boarded a troopship on June 8th, and crossed the Atlantic and landed safely in England on the 21st. He was assigned to the Artillery Holding Unit in Bordon, England. His stay with this unit was short. On July 1st, he was transferred to the 1st Survey Battery in Thursley. He remained with the Survey Battery until May 20th 1942, when he was transferred to the Canadian Artillery Reinforcement Unit. By then, he had been promoted to Acting Lance Sergeant (A/L/Sgt). On June 19th, he was, once again, transferred to the 1st Survey Regiment. He remained with this unit and, on June 25th 1943, he was promoted to Acting Battery Sergeant-Major. On January 17th 1944, Sergeant-Major Gleadall was Commissioned and reassigned to No.2 Canadian Artillery Reinforcement Unit. He underwent officer training and appointed a Lieutenant on August 6th 1944. On September 23rd, he married Joan Rowe at Stoke-Next-Guilford, Surrey, England. One month later, on October 26th, he was participating in a training exercise and while firing a PIAT anti-tank weapon, the projectile exploded prematurely causing massive trauma and injuries to Lieut. Gleadall. He was rushed to Basingstoke Neuro & Pastic Surgery Hospital, Royal Canadian Army Medical Corps, Basingstoke, Southampton, arriving at 1800hrs. Sadly, at 1915hrs, Lieutenant George Gleadall died of his injuries. He was buried in Plot 55, Row H, Grave 2, Brookwood Military Cemetery, Woking, Surrey, England.

Service number: D10744

Medals and Awards: Defence Medal, the Canadian Volunteer Service Medal and clasp and the War Medal 1939-45.

GOODFELLOW, Normand R. **Private**
1st Depot Bn **WWI**

Norman Robert Patton Goodfellow was born on December 4th 1894, in Arundel, son of Andrew, a farmer and Margaret Walker Patton. Norman was drafted into the Canadian Expeditionary Force, 1st Depot Battalion, 1st Quebec Regiment on July 16th 1918. Norman's mother had died in 1915 and his father, Andrew, had died on the 1st of July 1918. Sadly, Pte Norman Goodfellow died of pneumonia while on harvest leave, a few months after his father, on November 18th. He was buried on the 20th in the Arundel Methodist cemetery joining his parent's resting place. He had never left Canada.

Service number: 3087568
Medals and Awards: Nil

GRANGER, Eugène **Private**
22nd Bn **WWI**

Jean Eugène Granger was born in Farnham Quebec on February 8th 1899, son of Edouard and Henriette Jourdenais. In 1920, his sister Laura married Clodomir St-Jacques of Lachute. Eugène enlisted in the 41st Battalion, Canadian Expeditionary Force on August 30th 1915, in Quebec. At the time of his enlistment, he lied on his date of birth. The attestation paper reads that he was born in 1897. In fact Eugène was just 16 years old when he enlisted. He remained in Canada for the first few months of his enlistment. He arrived in England on October 28th having boarded the troopship S.S. Saxonia ten days earlier in Quebec. He remained in England with the 41st until his transfer to the 23rd Reserve Battalion on February 29th 1916. His stay with the 23rd was short lived as he was transferred to the 22nd Battalion on April 15th, and joined his new unit on the Western Front the next day. On July 15th, Eugène suffered a slight wound to his cheek while in the vicinity of St-Eloi, France and was evacuated to No.13 Stationary Hospital in Boulogne. He spent several months convalescing and rejoined his unit on September 20th. In the following November, Eugène contracted influenza and was once more removed from the frontline and sent to the military hospitals to recover. He returned to the 22nd Battalion on January 25th 1917. On August 15th 1917 at 0425hrs, the 22nd Battalion launched an attack from the trenches in the Cité St-Laurent sector of the front. This action was part of an attack by the Canadian Corps at Hill 70 in the area of Lens, France. Pte Eugène Granger was one of the approximately 100 casualties taken by the 22nd Battalion on that day. His body was never found. Eugène Granger was 18 years old when he gave his life for his country. He is commemorated on the Menin Gate Memorial in Ieper, West-Vlaanderen, Belgium.

Service number: 416886

Medals and Awards: British War Medal and Victory Medal (1914-1919)

GREEN, Arthur E. **Sapper**
C.R.T. **WWI**

Arthur Edward Green was born in Dartford, Kent, England on September 25th 1894, son of Frank and Clara Green. Arthur immigrated to Canada, arriving in Quebec on board the Empress of Ireland on June 25th 1909. His family followed him the next year and by 1911 they had settled in Chatham Township. Arthur started employment with the Canadian Explosives Limited ammunition plant in Brownsburg. On September 11th 1911, he married Bessie Florence Fisk in Lachute. This couple would have several children. On August 29th 1912, there was an explosion at the plant and Arthur was seriously injured, leaving him scarred. On March 5th 1916, Arthur enlisted with the 148th Overseas Battalion, Canadian Expeditionary Force in Lachute. After a medical review board, Arthur was discharged from the Army on April 24th, having been found unable to hold a rifle appropriately due to the injuries sustained in 1912. This would not leave Arthur out of the War. On July 6th, he re-enlisted, this time with No.1 Construction Battalion in Montreal. He remained in Canada for several months, until he boarded the troopship S.S. Northland, in Halifax, on September 13th, arriving safely in England on the 23rd. From England, Sapper Green was sent to France, arriving on October 26th. Upon reaching his unit in France, he got into trouble. On the 29th, he was sentenced to six days of Field Punishment number 1 for neglect of duty. On February 10th 1917, his unit changed designation and would therefore be known as the 1st Battalion, Canadian Railway Troops. Arthur had several medical issues ranging from boils on his legs, myalgia, dislocated and infected knees and trench fever. On August 7th 1918, he was transferred to the Canadian Forestry Corps. At War's end, Arthur was returned to Canada demobilizing in Kingston, Ontario on February 12th 1919. Afterwards, Arthur returned to Brownsburg with his family. Sadly, on December 28th 1924, Arthur died at the Montreal General Hospital of tuberculosis and was buried on the 31st in the Last Post section of the Mount-Royal Cemetery in Montreal. The records indicate that the cause of death was directly related to his military service.

Service numbers: 841694 and 1081677

Medals and Awards: British War Medal and Victory Medal (1914-1919)

GREEN, William **Unknown**
Unknown **WWII**

Unfortunetely, this soldier could not be positively identified. He is commemorated on the Brownsburg Memorial.

Service number: Unknown

Medals and Awards: Unknown

GREIG, William D. **Private**
R.H.R. **WWII**

William David Greig was born in Greece's Point on November 9th 1921, son of Donald Graham and Ellen Euphemia Watson. Donald Graham served during World War One with the Canadian Expeditionary Force as well as the Veteran's Guard in World War II. William David attended school until he was 13 years old, and occupied several positions for different employers in Montreal. On November 3rd 1939, he enlisted with the Canadian Army in Montreal and assigned to the 1st Battalion, The Black Watch (Royal Highland Regiment) of Canada. He saw service in Toronto, Valcartier and Botwood, Newfoundland. On August 22nd 1940, he boarded a troopship and left Canada enroute to the United Kingdom and the War, arriving safely in Gourock, Scotland on September 4th. He remained in England, training and preparing for the upcoming invasion of mainland Europe. On July 7th 1944, Pte Greig and the Black Watch landed in France. On August 5th, during an advance of the Black Watch towards the village of St-Andre-sur-Orne, Pte William David Greig was killed by enemy artillery. He was buried on the 14th, in Plot I, Row 3, Grave 14, Saint-Martin-de-Fontenay Cemetery. He was later exhumed and reburied in Plot I, Row G, Grave 12, Bretteville-sur-Laize Canadian War Cemetery, Calvados, France

Service number: D81790

Medals and Awards: 1939-45 Star, France and Germany Star, Defence Medal, the Canadian Volunteer Service Medal and clasp and the War Medal 1939-45.

GRUNDY, Gordon	**Private**
24th Bn	**WWI**

Gordon Grundy was born in Montreal on April 5th 1896, son of John, a stereotyper and Matilda Harrison. By 1911 this family was residing in Arundel. On October 26th 1914, Gordon enlisted with "B" Company, 24th Battalion, Canadian Expeditionary Force in Montreal. At the time of his enlistment, he reported being a driver and having served in the Active Militia with the 3rd Victoria Rifles of Canada. He remained in Canada until May 11th 1915, when he boarded the troopship S.S. Cameronia, arriving safely in England on the 20th. From England, he proceeded to France and landed on Continental Europe on September 15th. Once in France, he became ill and had to be brought out of the lines and sent back to England for treatment of a hernia. He eventually returned to the 24th on February 16th 1916. On June 19th, while the 24th was in the vicinity of Zillebeke, Belgium, he was critically wounded by shrapnel to both legs and was evacuated to No.3 Canadian Casualty Clearing Station. Pte Gordon Grundy died the next day at 2315hrs. He was buried in Plot VIII, Row B, Grave 5A, Lijssenthoek Military Cemetery, West-Vlaanderen, Belgium.

Service number: 65399

Medals and Awards: 1914-15 Star, British War Medal and Victory Medal (1914-1919).

HALL, George L. **F/Sergeant**
R.C.A.F. **WWII**

LAC/BAC

George Langley Hall was born in Lachine, Quebec on January 29th 1911, son of Thomas Percy, an electrical mechanic, and Nellie Bodfish. Nellie passed away in 1955 having resided in St-Andrews East and Thomas Percy died in 1964 and was residing in Brownsburg. Both are buried in the St-Andrews East Protestant cemetery. George attended the Lachine High School from 1918 to 1929 and then went to work as a clerk, for the Royal Bank of Canada in Montreal until 1938. He was then employed by the Dominion Bridge Company in Lachine as a clerk and checker. George enlisted with the Royal Canadian Air Force on June 27th 1941, in Montreal and was taken on strength with No.4 Manning Depot in St-Hubert, Quebec until August 10th, when he was sent to No.8 Service Flying Training School in Moncton, New Brunswick. Then, he was sent to No.3 Initial Training School in Victoriaville,

Quebec for further training. From there, on Deember 21st he was sent to No.8 Air Observer School in L'Ancienne-Lorette, Quebec, remaining there for three months. On March 29th 1942, he was assigned to No.9 Bombing and Gunnery School in Mont-Joli, Quebec. His training wasn't complete since, on May 24th, he was sent to No.1 Air Navigation School in Rivers, Manitoba. He left Canada on September 25th, enroute for the United Kingdom and the War. He arrived safely on October 7th, and assigned to No.3 Personnel Reception Centre in Bournemouth, England the next day. On November 4th, he was transferred to No.22 Operational Training Unit in Wellesbourne, England. On January 29th 1943, F/Sgt Hall was a crew member on board Wellington X bomber, number HF650, which took off for a night sortie. The bomber stalled at 1000 feet and crashed near Epwell, England. Unfortunately, F/Sgt George Langley Hall did not survive the crash and, on February 4th, was buried in Section K, Grave 38, Moreton-in-Marsh New Cemetery, Gloucestershire, England.

Service number: R108359

Medals and Awards: Defence Medal, the Canadian Volunteer Service Medal and clasp and the War Medal 1939-45.

HALSEY, James Charles **Major**
102nd Bn **WWI**

James Charles Halsey was born in Carillon on September 7th 1882, son of John Edward and Margaret Beaton. James Charles remained in Carillon but by 1901 found himself in the Kootenay area of British Columbia working as a powder trader. James Charles remained in British Columbia and on October 13th 1911, married

Hester May Kergin in Prince Rupert. By this time he was working as a real estate agent. James Charles enlisted with the 102nd Battalion of the Canadian Expeditionary Force on May 1st 1916. He was no stranger to the military as he had served with the 68th Earl Grey's Own prior to this enlistment. He remained in Canada for a few months then boarded the troopship S.S. Empress of Britain on June 18th 1916, landing in England on the 27th. He remained in England until he crossed to Continental Europe and reached France on August 2nd. By mid December 1916 James Charles became very ill and had to be admitted to military hospitals. He had contracted tuberculosis while in France. His military career was over. He remained in hospitals, at first in France, and then in England until July 20th 1917, when he boarded the ship S.S. Missanabie and headed back home having been found medically unfit for further service in the C.E.F. Back in British Columbia he was admitted to a sanatorium in Balfour, B.C., for treatment. The treatment failed and sadly, on August 22nd 1918, Major James Charles Halsey died. He was buried in Military Plot B4, Grave 6, Nelson Memorial Park cemetery, Nelson, British Columbia.

Service number: Major

Medals and Awards: British War Medal and Victory Medal (1914-1919)

HAMMOND, Henry L. **Private**
P.P.C.L.I. **WWI**

Henry Leggo Hammond was born in Chatham Township on June 16th 1896, son of Henry Richard, a farmer and Edith Charlotte Leggo. Henry Leggo remained with his family in his earlier years. He started his career with the Bank of Ottawa on September 4th 1912, at the Lachute Branch. By 1915, he was residing at 127 Drummond Street in Montreal working as a bank clerk at the Bank of Ottawa. On September 24th 1915, he enlisted in the 4th Overseas Universities Company, C.E.F. He had served in the militia, prior to his enlistment, with the 55th Irish Rangers Regiment. He left Canada on November 27th, when he boarded the troopship S.S. Lapland in Halifax. He arrived in England on December 7th, and went directly to Shorncliffe. He remained in England until he was transferred to the P.P.C.L.I. on April 23rd 1916, arriving at the Front the next day. He was temporarily assigned to the 7th Field Company, Canadian Engineers on February 13th 1917, and this assignment lasted several months with brief periods of returning to his Battalion. During this time, he would have been employed at repairing trenches, extending dugouts and other tasks as assigned. On September 1st, he rejoined his unit in the field. On October 10th, he got in a bit of trouble as he was sentenced to three days of Field Punishment #1 for losing his helmet. This didn't curtail his chances at a promotion since, on June 18th 1918, he was promoted to Corporal. On September 30th 1918, at about 0600hrs, the P.P.C.L.I. launched an attack towards the village of Tilloy in France. Corporal Henry Leggo Hammond was killed in action during this attack. He was buried in Row C, Grave 21, Mill Switch British Cemetery, Tilloy-Les-Cambrai, Nord, France.

Service number: 475361

Medals and Awards: British War Medal and Victory Medal (1914-1919)

HAWKINS, Thomas J. **Private**
50th Bn **WWI**

Thomas John Hawkins was born in Montreal around 1863, the son of Mathew and Ellen Barry. Prior to 1860, his father, who was a Corporal in the Royal Canadian Rifles Regiment, came to Canada and was stationed in Quebec City. By 1871, Mathew was a pensioner and they were residing in the Windsor area of Richmond County, Quebec. In 1874, this family moved to the Grenville area. Thomas John enlisted with the 138th Overseas Battalion of the C.E.F. on January 17th 1916, in Edmonton Alberta. At the time of his enlistment, he was residing in Wetaskiwin, Alberta, worked as a steam shovel engineer and declared having been born on the 9th of November 1882 therefore lying about his true age which was about 53 years old. He left Canada, sailing for England on board the troopship S.S. Olympic on August 22nd, and arrived safely on the 30th. He remained in England, being transferred to other units until he crossed into France on June 29th 1917, and landed at Boulogne. Once in France, he was posted to No.5 Canadian Area Employment Company where he would have been assigned duties such as orderly, batman, clerk or cook. By 1918, the Army had caught on and was well aware that Pte Hawkins was well into his fifties. He was returned to England on February 19th, and assigned to the Alberta Regimental Depot in Bramshott. He was returned to Canada on board the troopship S.S. Mauritania on May 20th, and was discharged from the C.E.F., having been found medically unfit for further service, on July 14th, in Calgary Alberta. Thomas John suffered from debility myalgia while he was in the military. On October 7th 1928, he died at Ste Anne de Bellevue of myocarditis and of pre-senility. The attending physician wrote in his death card that this was a direct result of his service in the War. He was buried in St-Mathews cemetery in Grenville.

Service number: 811771

Medals and Awards: British War Medal and Victory Medal (1914-1919)

HOWARD, Arthur "Gat" L. **T/Major**
Cdn Scouts **Boer War**

Courtesy Gina Sammis

Arthur Lockhart Howard was born in New Hampshire, United States, in 1846, son of Lockhart and Jane Fuller. His childhood is unknown. It appears that Arthur enlisted with the 1st U.S. Cavalry on April 20th 1867, remaining with this unit until his discharge on June 30th 1871. On December 25th 1873, Arthur married Sarah E. Newgeon in New Haven, Connecticut. In 1880, he was residing in New Haven, and was employed as a cartridge maker. In 1885, now Captain Howard, who was an officer in the Connecticut National Guard, was assigned to the Canadian Expedition aimed at stopping the Louis Riel Rebellion. He was a technical advisor to the new Gatling guns, which had been lent to the Canadian Forces while the ones requested by the Canadian government were being built. It was during the battle of Batoche that, Capt. Howard and his guns saw action. Major General Middleton described this officer's bravery: "Capt. Howard, the instructor in the use of the weapon, showed great gallantry and cool courage." By 1891, he was residing in

Chatham Township with his children, and was the manager of the Dominion Cartridge Company in Brownsburg, employing some 70 people. On January 9th 1895, in New Haven, Arthur married Margaret Green from Brownsburg, having divorced Sarah in 1888. In 1899, Britain found herself at war with the Boer Republics in South Africa. Arthur was commissioned a Lieutenant in the Canadian Army Reserve of officers and went to South Africa as a machine gun officer. On January 21st 1900, Lieut. Howard left Halifax on board the S.S. Laurentian, and sailed for South Africa, arriving safely in Capetown, on February 16th. Once in South Africa, he was assigned to the 2nd Canadian Mounted Rifles and then to the Royal Canadian Dragoons. Lieut. Howard had a reputation for his bravery in action. By the end of 1900, Lieutenant Howard was promoted to Temporary Major and assigned the task of raising a Scout unit which would be known as the Canadian Scouts or Howard's Scouts. Major Howard was an officer who led from the front. On February 17th 1901, Major Arthur Howard was killed in action when his unit ran into Boer Commandos, while en route to Schwaabe's Store, towards the Swaziland border. His death is subject of much debate. Some reports indicate he had been shot in a fair fight but other eyewitnesses reported that Major Howard had surrendered to a Boer force along with another soldier and a native scout and all three had been murdered. For his service in South Africa, he was twice mentioned in Despatches. Lord Kitchener said it well on his despatch of May 8th, 1901: "has been repeatedly brought to my notice for acts of gallantry". Major Howard was awarded the Distinguished Service Order, posthumously, which was gazetted on September 27th, 1901. He is commemorated in the Wakkerstroom Garden of Remembrance in South Africa.

Service Number: Lieutenant

Medals and Awards: Companion of the Distinguished Service Order (DSO), North West Canada Medal with Saskatchewan bar, Queen's South Africa Medal with Johannesburg, Diamond Hill, Belfast, Cape Colony, Orange Free State clasps.

HUTCHEON, Alexander **Private**
42nd Bn **WWI**

Alexander Duncan Hutcheon was born in Aberdeen, Scotland on October 27th 1890, the son of William and Mary Ann McLeod. By 1911 he had immigrated to Canada and was working on a farm in St-Canut, Quebec. He enlisted with "D" Company, 42nd Battalion, C.E.F. in Montreal on May 21st 1915. He proceeded to England on June 10th, having boarded the troopship S.S. Hesperian and arrived on the 19th. He remained in England until he crossed into France on October 9th. On June 2nd 1916, the Germans launched an attack aimed at Mount Sorrel, which was defended by the Canadian Corps. On June 8th, during this fearsome combat, Pte Alexander Hutcheon suffered a gunshot wound to his left ankle and, as a result, was taken out of the line and eventually evacuated to the Ontario Military Hospital in Orpington, England. After his stay at the hospital, he was sent to a Convalescent Hospital in order to recuperate prior to rejoining his unit. On July 29th, he was assigned to the 92nd Battalion and returned to his unit, the 42nd, on September 5th. It was while in the lines, on or about October 10th 1916, that Alexander Duncan was shot in the back of the neck. He died on that day at No.49 Casualty Clearing Station. He was buried in Plot IV, Row A, Grave 13, Contay British Cemetery, Contay, Somme, France.

Service number: 418951

Medals and Awards: 1914-1915 Star, British War Medal and Victory Medal (1914-1919)

HUTCHINSON, James W. 73rd Bn **Private WWI**

Short history 73rd Battalion

James Waldron Hutchinson was born on July 3rd 1873, in Bridgetown, Barbados. Prior to immigrating to Canada, he had served six years with the Trinidad Light Infantry. On August 17th 1915, he enlisted in Montreal with No.11 Platoon, "C" Company of the 73rd Battalion, C.E.F. After James' first wife, Amy Agatha Moze, died in 1912, he remarried to Elizabeth Ann Waterson in St-Lambert, Quebec on February 5th, 1916. His family moved to Lachute sometime after he left for the War. He left his new wife and children in Canada and sailed for England with his Battalion on the troopship R.M.S. Adriatic on March 31st 1916, and arrived on the 9th of April in Liverpool. He spent a few months in England and crossed the Channel on August 13th and landed at Le Havre, France. On the morning of November 13th 1916, he was hit in the right shoulder and right breast by enemy shrapnel and killed, while in Regina Trench, Courcelette, France. He is remembered with Honour on the Vimy Memorial, Pas-de-Calais, France.

Service number: 132118

Medals and Awards: British War Medal and Victory Medal (1914-1919)

JONES, William D. **Corporal**
4th P.L.D.G. **WWII**

William David Jones was born in Montreal, Quebec on January 8th 1911, son of Frederick and Sarah Slade. His mother died in 1914 and his father was killed in 1918, serving with the Canadian Expeditionary Force in Europe, during World War One. William and his sibblings were taken in by David Maxwell of Montreal. By 1935, this family was residing in the St Jerusalem parish area. He attended school in Montreal, completing one year of high school and two years of technical school, leaving at age 15. In 1938, he started employment with the Dominion Oil Cloth Company in Montreal, as a varnish maker. On July 18th 1940, he enlisted in the Canadian Army in Montreal. At that time, he reported having previous military service with the Canadian Garrison Artillery, the Black Watch and the 17th Duke of York Royal Canadian Hussars. He was immediately taken on strength with the 3rd Canadian Motorcycle Regiment in Montreal, and promoted to Corporal. On February 26th 1941, he was transferred to the 17th D.Y.R.C.H. and sent to Camp Debert, Nova Scotia. His rise in the ranks continued and he was promoted to Sergeant on July 15th. On August 23rd, he embarked on a troopship and crossed the Atlantic, arriving safely in the United Kingdom on September 2nd. On November 27th, he was assigned to the 7th Reconnaissance Regiment. On February 23rd 1942, he reverted to the rank of Corporal at his own request. He remained in the United Kingdom until October 26th 1943, when he boarded a troopship and left for the Mediterranean Theatre of War, arriving safely on November 9th. He was assigned to the 4th Princess Louise Dragoon Guards on July 25th 1944, after having spent some time with the 4th Reconnaissance. On September 1st 1944, Cpl

William David Jones was killed in action during fierce fighting in the Tomba di Pesaro area. He was temporarily buried in Grave F 6, Gothic Line III, 5th Canadian Armored Division cemetery. He was later exhumed and reburied in Plot IV, Row J, Grave 14, Montecchio War Cemetery, Italy.

Service number: D3131

Medals and Awards: 1939-45 Star, Italy Star, Defence Medal, the Canadian Volunteer Service Medal and clasp and the War Medal 1939-45.

JOSS, Harry Edwin **Private**
73rd Bn **WWI**

Short history 73rd Battalion

Harry Edwin Joss was born in Lachute on October 15th 1894, son of George, a contractor and Elizabeth Stalker. Harry's father, George, died in Lachute in 1907. On March 1st 1913, Harry began working as a bank clerk at the Lachute Branch of the Bank of Ottawa. Harry Edwin enlisted in Montreal with No.13 Platoon, "D" Company, 73rd Battalion, C.E.F. on September 15th 1915. He remained in Canada until he crossed the Atlantic bound for England and the War on the troopship R.M.S. Adriatic on March 31st 1916, and arrived on the 9th of April in Liverpool. In May he was promoted to the rank of Lance/Corporal until June 23rd, when he reverted to the rank of Private at his own request. On August 12th, he crossed into France, landing on the 13th at Le Havre. His Battalion joined the 4th Division of the Canadian Corps in the frontlines. On October 16th

1916, while at Tara Hill Camp, France, he was shot in the face and, as a result, died of wounds at No.49 Casualty Clearing Station. He was buried in Plot III, Row C, Grave 19, Contay British Cemetery, Contay, Somme, France.

Service number: 132503

Medals and Awards: British War Medal and Victory Medal (1914-1919)

KENNEDY, Ward **A/Seaman**
Merchant Marine **WWII**

Ernest Ward Kennedy was born in Grenville on February 22nd 1919, son of Ernest Ward, a farmer, and Lily May Kennedy. Very little is known of this mariner. On August 29th 1941, he signed an engagement as an able seaman on board the S.S. Empire Eland. This ship was part of convoy ON14 en route from Liverpool, England to Tampa, Florida. On September 15th 1941, at 2348hrs, the Empire Eland was struck by a torpedo fired from the German submarine U-94 south-east of Cape Farewell in the North Atlantic. A second torpedo hit at 0030hrs on the 16th sank the ship. All hands were lost. Able/Seaman Ward Kennedy is commemorated on the Halifax Memorial, Halifax, Nova-Scotia.

KIRKPATRICK, Ernest L. **Gunner**
3rd Brig, C.F.A. **WWI**

Ernest Leslie Kirkpatrick (Kilpatrick) was born on March 29th 1898, in Lachute, son of John, a carter by trade, and Mary Jane Arnold. By 1911, he was residing on Ontario Street in Montreal with his mother. On August 29th 1916, he enlisted with "C" Battery, Royal Canadian Horse

Artillery (R.C.H.A.), C.E.F., in Kingston, Ontario. At the time of his enlistment, he was still residing in Montreal and was employed as an electrician. On November 23rd, he boarded the troopship S.S. Mauretania and arrived in Liverpool, England on the 30th. On his arrival, he was transferred to the Reserve Artillery Brigade in Shorncliffe. On August 2nd, he crossed into France and was assigned to the 4th Canadian Divisional Ammunition Column. On October 20th 1917, while in the vicinity of Ypres, Belgium, he was gassed by an enemy shell. He was treated at No.11 Australian Field Ambulance and returned to duty on the same day. From the 4th C.D.A.C., he was transferred to the 3rd Brigade, Canadian Field Artillery on October 23rd. On September 27th 1918, the 3rd Brigade was assigned to support the Canadian Corps on its assault of the Canal du Nord and Bourlon Wood. Gunner Kirkpatrick was killed by an enemy shell while on outpost duty near Bourlon Wood while the Brigade was in the area of Moeuvres, France. He was buried in Plot I, Row B, Grave 18, Bourlon Wood Cemetery, Pas-de-Calais, France.

Service number: 349303

Medals and Awards: British War Medal and Victory Medal (1914-1919)

LAFONTAINE, Emile **Private**
Régt. Maison. **WWII**

Joseph Emile Roger Lafontaine was born in Hawkesbury, Ontario on August 29th 1924, son of William and Victoria Lécuyer. He resided in Hawkesbury for the first part of his life, attending school until he was 16 years old. After school in 1940, he began working as a lumberman for the Intercity Lumber Company out of Hawkesbury.

By 1943, this family was residing in St-Michel-de-Wentworth in Argenteuil County, Quebec. On September 30th 1943, he enlisted with the Canadian Army in Kingston, Ontario and was taken on strength with No.3A District Depot, awaiting his training as an infantryman. On October 22nd, he was then sent to No.45 Basic Training Centre in Sorel, Quebec. On May 1st 1944, he was transferred to the Régiment de Joliette and was stationed in Rimouski, Quebec until July 17th, when he was sent to No.1 Transit Camp in Windsor, Nova-Scotia, awaiting a transport which would bring him to the United Kingdom. On October 14th, he boarded a troopship and crossed the Atlantic, reaching the United Kingdom safely on the 21st. He was immediately taken on strength with No.4 Canadian Infantry Reinforcement Unit and received further training. Pte Lafontaine was sent to mainland Europe on December 2nd and, on the 9th, joined his new unit, the Régiment de Maisonneuve. On February 27th 1945, Pte Emile Lafontaine was killed in action in Germany. He was initially buried in Bedburg cemetery and was later exhumed and reburied in Plot X, Row G, Grave 8, Groesbeek Canadian Military Cemetery, Gelderland, Holland.

Service number: C116014

Medals and Awards: 1939-45 Star, France and Germany Star, the Canadian Volunteer Service Medal and clasp and the War Medal 1939-45.

LAFOREST, Wilfrid **Private**
22nd Bn **WWI**

Wilfrid Laforest was born Joseph Wilbrod Roméo Laforest in Lachute, on March 2nd 1900, son of Magloire, a laborer and Marie Louise Brisson. His mother died on March 1st 1905, and his father remarried in 1906 with Célanire Brisson. In 1911, Wilbrod was working as a domestic in St-Hermas. On April 11th 1916, he enlisted with the 163rd Overseas Battalion, C.E.F. and was now residing in Brownsburg. He boarded the troopship S.S. Metagama and arrived in England on December 6th. He remained in England and was transferred to the 10th Reserve Battalion on January 7th 1917. On August 15th, he was transferred to the Boys Battalion, more than likely due to the fact he was 17 years old. On May 30th 1918, he was returned to the 10th Reserve Battalion. On June 26th, he was finally transferred to the 22nd Battalion and joined his unit in the field. On August 16th 1918, during a minor operation in which the 22nd advanced some 500 yards in trenches North of Chilly, France, Pte Laforest was instantly killed by enemy shell fire. He was only 18 years old. He was buried in Row B, Grave 16, in the Vrely Communal Cemetery Extension, Somme, France.

Service number: 660957

Medals and Awards: British War Medal and Victory Medal (1914-1919)

LAMBERTSON, John M. **2nd/Lieut.**
116th U.S. Inf. **WWII**

John Moreland Lambertson was born in Toronto, Ontario on February 5th 1921, son of John and Margaret Moreland. In 1921, John and his family were residing in Montreal. Sometime after 1921, the Lambertsons moved to Brownsburg and John attended Public School there. By 1940, John and his family had moved to Ocean Township, New-Jersey, United States, and he was working as an usher in a theater. On May 14th 1942, John enlisted as a Private, with HQ Company, 1st Battalion, 116th Infantry Regiment, 29th Infantry Division in Ashbury Park, New-Jersey. Pte Lambertson left the United States and made the crossing to Europe, reaching the United Kingdom safely. It is unclear if John participated in the Normandy Invasion of June 6th 1944, but the 29th Division was heavily engaged against German Forces in Europe. On November 1st 1944, he received a battlefield commission, being promoted to 2nd Lieutenant. Sadly, just 20 days later, Lt John Moreland Lambertson was killed in action in Germany. His place of burial is unknown.

Service number: 01996533

Medals and Awards: Purple Heart, European-African-Middle-Eastern Campaign Medal, World War II Victory Medal.

LANGEVIN, Stéphane **M/Corporal**
12e R.B.C. **United Nations**

LAC/BAC

Luc Pierre Stéphane Langevin was born on August 31st 1965, son of Roger and Marjolaine Modérie. Stéphane attended school, graduating from grade 12 in 1983. On May 25th 1987, he enlisted with the Canadian Armed Forces in St-Jerome, Quebec and, on June 7th, began his recruit training in C.F.B. St-Jean, Quebec. Once completed, on August 15th, he was sent to C.F.B. Valcartier and posted to the 12e Régiment Blindé du Canada. Stéphane was promoted to Corporal on June 7th 1990. On August 19th, Cpl Langevin was sent on his first United Nations Peacekeeping Mission on the island of Cyprus. On May 10th 1991, after his return, he was promoted to Master Corporal. After Cyprus, he was sent to Bosnia and Herzegovina in 1993. It was during this tour in Bosnia that, on November 29th 1993, M/Cpl Stéphane Langevin was killed when, the Cougar armoured vehicle he was a passenger in, was involved in a road accident, near the city of Zenica. He was buried in Row I, Grave 3, St-André d'Argenteuil Cemetery, Quebec.

Service number: B85 139 991

Medals and Awards: Canadian Peacekeeping Service Medal, United Nations Forces in Cyprus (UNFICYP), Dag Hammarskjöld Medal.

LAPOINTE, Napoléon **Private**
22nd Bn **WWI**

Joseph Napoléon Lapointe was born in Lachute on April 17th 1885, son of Joseph and Philomène Papineau. Napoléon's father, Joseph died in 1899 and his mother remarried in 1906. Napoléon enlisted with the 22nd Battalion, C.E.F. in St-Jean, Quebec on December 4th 1914. He remained in Canada until he sailed for England on May 20th 1915, leaving Halifax on board the troopship S.S. Saxonia, arriving on the 29th. He remained in England with his Battalion, until September 15th, when he went to France. In March 1916, he had several stays in military hospitals for different illnesses. On May 12th, he was sentenced to 10 days field punishment #1 for having been absent without leave. On May 18th 1916, only six days after being sentenced to field punishment, while on duty in the trenches of St-Eloi, he was struck and instantly killed by splinters from an enemy trench mortar which burst in the trenches close to him. He was buried in Plot III, Row C, Grave 7, of the Elzenwalle Brasserie Cemetery, West-Vlaanderen, Belgium.

Service number: 62106

Medals and Awards: 1914-1915 Star, British War Medal and Victory Medal (1914-1919)

LEMAY, Jean-Paul **Sergeant**
R22eR **WWII**

Joseph Jean Paul Lemay was born in Montreal on May 15th 1920, son of Maria Lemay. His father is unknown. Jean Paul grew up in Grenville and, with his mother, resided with Hormidas Lemay, Maria's father. He attended school until grade eight. Prior to his enlistment he was employed as a salesman at various locations. Jean-Paul enlisted with the Canadian Army on September 7th 1939, in Montreal, and was immediately taken on strength with the Fusiliers Mont-Royal. He remained in Canada, training, until June 30th 1940, when he left Canada and proceeded to Iceland, for garrison duty, disembarking in Reykjavik on July 7th. He remained in Iceland until October 26th, and proceeded to Scotland, arriving safely in Gourock on November 3rd. The next day he was on duty in Aldershot, England. He was promoted to corporal on September 10th 1941 and to sergeant on April 28th 1943. His mother, Maria, had died on March 29th 1943, while Jean-Paul was in the United Kingdom. On September 25th, he boarded a troopship in the United Kingdom and was sent to the Mediterranean Theater of Operations, arriving safely in Italy on October 16th. Sgt Lemay was transferred to the Royal 22e Régiment on November 13th. On December 20th 1943, Sgt Jean-Paul Lemay was killed in action in the vicinity of Ortona, Italy. He was temporarily buried in the Casa Berardi Cemetery, Chieti, Italy and was later exhumed and reburied in Plot II, Row E, Grave 10, Moro River Canadian War Cemetery, Italy.

Service number: D61006

Medals and Awards: 1939-45 Star, Italy Star, Defence Medal, the Canadian Volunteer Service Medal and clasp and the War Medal 1939-45.

LE ROY, John McCallum **Private**
5th Bn **WWI**

John McCallum Le Roy was born on October 5th 1886, in St-Andrews East, son of Archibald, a farmer and Susannah MacGregor. He and his family moved around. In 1901, they were residing in East Hawkesbury and by 1906 they had moved and were residing in Saskatchewan. He enlisted in Humboldt, Saskatchewan on January 16th 1915, with the 53rd Battalion, C.E.F. Prior to this, he had served 12 months with the 90th Regiment out of Winnipeg, Manitoba. His brother, Charles William, would be drafted on June 11th 1918 and would survive the War. On June 17th, John McCallum boarded the troopship S.S. Scandinavian and crossed to England and the War. On the 27th, he was transferred to the 32nd Reserve Battalion but didn't remain with this unit for long. On August 3rd, he was transferred to the 5th Battalion and landed in France. On June 6th 1916, while his Battalion was in the trenches near Hill 60, Belgium, he was wounded in his right thigh. He was withdrawn from the front and evacuated to England for treatment. This was followed by an operation and convalescence. He was able to join the 11th Reserve Battalion on September 16th, in Shorncliffe. On October 9th, he rejoined his Battalion, the 5th, in the frontlines. At 0425hrs, on April 28th 1917, the 5th Battalion launched an attack in the vicinity of Arleux, France. The Battalion suffered 240 casualties in this attack and Pte Le Roy was one of them, having been hit by shrapnel to his back and thigh. He died at No.3 Canadian Field Ambulance. He was buried in Row L, Grave 22, in the Ste. Catherine British Cemetery, Pas-de-Calais, France.

Service number: A40239 and 440239

Medals and Awards: 1914-1915 Star, British War Medal and Victory Medal (1914-1919)

LEROY, Osmond Edgar **Captain**
46th Bn **WWI**

McGill Honour Roll 1914-1918

Osmond Edgar Leroy was born in St-Andrews East on January 28th 1873, son of Alexander, a blacksmith and Hannah Albright. He was John McCallum Leroy's cousin, since both their fathers, Alexander and Archibald were brothers. By 1891, Osmond was a school teacher and still residing in St-Andrews East. On July 28th 1893, he was commissioned as a Second Lieutenant with the 11th Battalion, Argenteuil Rangers and served three years as such. He attended McGill University and graduated with a Bachelor of Arts in 1895. He continued his studies and obtained his Masters in Sciences in 1902, and became a geologist. He was employed by the Geological Survey Department of Canada and kept busy by surveying in British Columbia for several years. He was the author of several books on geology in Quebec, Ontario, and British Columbia. Osmond Edgar enlisted with the 196th Battalion on February 16th 1916, in Vancouver, British Columbia. He had been commissioned in the Active Militia with the 72nd Regiment on October 1st 1915. He remained in Canada until November 1st, when he boarded the troopship S.S. Southland in Halifax bound for England. He arrived safely in Liverpool 10 days later. On December 31st, he was transferred to the 19th Reserve Battalion since his Battalion, the 196th, was being absorbed by the 19th. He remained in England for several months until he arrived in France on May 29th 1917, and joined up with his new unit, the 46th Battalion. On the morning of October 26th, the Canadian Corps launched an attack against the Germans at Passchendaele, Belgium. The 46th Battalion took part in this attack and proceeded in capturing their assigned objective, but had to withdraw due to a German counter-attack later in the day. The battlefield was a quagmire of mud and the soldiers caught in it found movement very difficult if not impossible. Capt Osmond Edgar Leroy, while going over the top, was severely wounded by an enemy shell in the abdomen and neck. He was treated in the field then evacuated to No.44 Casualty Clearing Station where, two days later, he died. The 46th Battalion's war diarist reported that they had suffered an astonishing 402 combat casualties in this attack. Capt Osmond Edgar Leroy was buried in Plot VI, Row A, Grave 4, Nine Elms British Cemetery, West-Vlaanderen, Belgium.

Service number: Captain

Medals and Awards: British War Medal and Victory Medal (1914-1919)

LEWIS, Albert H. **Private**
P.P.C.L.I. **WWI**

Albert Herbert Lewis was born in Falmouth, Cornwall, England, on January 14th 1892, son of Albert and Jessie Truscott. He remained in England until he immigrated to Canada and arrived in Montreal on board the ship S.S. Royal George on April 27th 1911, along with his younger brother, Stanley, wanting to join their father. His mother resided in Montreal but by 1920 was residing in Morin-Heights. On November 27th 1915, he enlisted with the 5th Overseas Universities Company, C.E.F., in Montreal. At the time of his enlistment, he declared having served three years with the Territorial Royal Engineers from 1907 to 1910, and being a fireman by trade. He remained in Canada until he boarded the troopship S.S. Olympic on April 1st 1916, arriving in England on the 11th. On his arrival he was taken on strength with the 11th Battalion but this was for a short period, since, on June 6th, he was transferred to the P.P.C.L.I. and arrived in France and with his Battalion on the 7th. On November 8th 1916, while in the vicinity of Mont St-Eloi, France, he was slightly wounded to the head and was withdrawn from the lines and sent to No.9 Canadian Field Ambulance for treatment and to the Divisional Rest Station on the same day. He was able to rejoin his unit in the field on the 15th. Albert's War continued and on July 2nd 1917, this time in the Carency, France sector, he was again wounded to the head and sent to the rear for treatment at No.8 Canadian Field Ambulance, rejoining the Battalion on the 10th. On August 26th 1917, Pte Albert Lewis was killed in action while in trenches north of Lens, France. The war diarist reports that the scout section was wiped out by an enemy shell. The P.P.C.L.I. suffered six killed and 70 wounded on that day.

Pte Albert Herbert Lewis is commemorated on the Vimy Memorial, Pas-de-Calais, France.

Service number: 487285

Medals and Awards: British War Medal and Victory Medal (1914-1919)

LIPSCOMBE, William H. R.N. **Chief Stoker WWII**

Courtesy Tom Liscombe

William Henry Lipscombe was born in Heveningham, Suffolk, England, on May 30th 1901, son of George, a retired Royal Navy sailor, and Edith Bonham Belcher. On May 30th 1919, he enlisted in the Royal Navy as a stoker, serving on numerous training and operational ships. William's family immigrated to Canada in 1923, having boarded the ship S.S. Melita in Portsmouth, England on July 5th, arriving in Quebec on the 13th, settling in Montreal. William remained in England and visited his family in Quebec on at least two occasions; in 1931 and in 1937. On September 18th 1937, William Henry married Lily Elizabeth Peckham in Bedhampton, England. By 1940, William Henry's parents were residing in St-Andrews East. On May 22nd 1941, Chief Stoker William Henry Lipscombe was on board H.M.S. Fiji, which was part of a Battle Fleet in the area of Crete. The Fleet was attacked relentlessly by German aircrafts and Fiji's companion ship, the cruiser H.M.S. Gloucester was sunk. For hours, Fiji fought back the air attacks until 1915hrs, when she was hit by a 500lbs bomb. This hit crippled the ship and she was hit again by bombs dropped from a single German aircraft. One hour later, H.M.S. Fiji sunk. Chief/Stoker Lipscombe's body was never recovered. He is commemorated on Panel 53, Column 3, Portsmouth Naval Memorial, Hampshire, United Kingdom.

Service Number: K56733

Medals and Awards: 1939-1945 Star, Atlantic Star, Africa Star, 1939-1945 War Medal, Royal Naval Long Service and Good Conduct Medal

LITTLE, Leonard J. **Private**
42nd Bn **WWI**

Leonard John Little was born in Grenville, on July 16th 1897, son of Walter and Carrie Emma Cousins. By 1911, John was residing in Grenville Township with his sister, Bella, his mother and his maternal grandfather, Richard Cousins. Leonard John's mother died of tuberculosis in February 1916. He enlisted with the 148th Overseas Battalion on June 26th 1916 in Montreal. On his enlistment paper, he is listed as being a scale man by trade and residing at 258 Guy Street, Montreal. He remained in Canada for several months until he boarded the troopship S.S. Laconia in Halifax on September 26th, bound for England and the War. On October 6th, he arrived safely in England and disembarked in Liverpool. For the next several months, he remained in England, being transferred on January 8th 1917, to the 20th Reserve Battalion in Shoreham, England. On June 25th, he was transferred to the 42nd Battalion and arrived in France and with his new Battalion the next day. He spent several months in and out of hospitals for treatment of ingrown toe nails. On August

26th 1918, the 42nd Battalion was part of a major offensive which would later be known as the Breaking of the Hindenburg Line. Pte Leonard John Little was instantly killed by an enemy sniper while bombing up "Knife" Trench, near Monchy on the Arras Front in France. He is commemorated on the Vimy Memorial, Pas-de-Calais, France.

Service number: 842241

Medals and Awards: British War Medal and Victory Medal (1914-1919)

LLOYD, George **Private**
60th Bn **WWI**

George Emmanuel Lloyd was born in Bristol, England on April 9th 1890, son of William and Anne Jane Reece. In 1911, he was residing in Montreal and worked as a tinsmith. On October 4th, he married Agnes Caroline Clark in Cushing. George enlisted with "B" Company, 60th Battalion, C.E.F., in Montreal on August 21st 1915. Prior to his enlistment, he had served two years with the Canadian Militia with the 3rd Victoria Rifles out of Montreal. He remained in Canada until November 6th, when he boarded the troopship S.S. Scandinavian bound for England, arriving safely on the 16th. He remained in England until he crossed and landed in Le Havre, France on February 22nd 1916. Four days later he was deprived of nine days pay for having been absent without leave. On June 3rd 1916, the 60th Battalion was ordered to support other units, in a counter-attack, in order to re-capture trenches which had been captured by the Germans. Pte George Lloyd was killed in that action east of Zillebeke, Belgium. He is commemorated on the

Ypres (Menin Gate) Memorial, West-Vlaanderen, Belgium.

Service number: 458555

Medals and Awards: British War Medal and Victory Medal (1914-1919)

LUMMIS, James C. **F/Officer**
R.C.A.F. **WWII**

LAC/BAC

James Cornwallis Lummis was born in Lakefield, on September 21st 1920, son of Wallace James Hamilton, an Anglican minister and Sarah Agnes Millar. James attended Morin Heights Intermediate School from 1927 to 1936 then Montreal High School from 1936 to 1940. His father passed away in 1939. In 1940 he was employed as a tinsmith for Liquid Carbonic in Montreal and from 1940 to 1942 as a parachute corder for Switlik Canadian Parachute also in Montreal. He enlisted with the Royal Canadian Air Force on August 17th 1942. By this time he was residing on 5th Avenue in Rosemont, Quebec. James was taken on strength with No.5 Manning Depot in Lachine, Quebec on the same day until September 26th, when he was sent to No.4 Manning Depot in Quebec City. On December 6th, he was sent to No.3 Initial Training School in Victoriaville, Quebec for the start of his flight training. He remained in Victoriaville until March 7th 1943, when he attended No.1 Bombing and Gunnery School in Jarvis, Ontario. On May 30th, he was then sent to No.4 Air Observer School in London, Ontario. James was commissioned as a

Pilot Officer on July 9th. On August 3rd, he boarded a troopship in New-York and crossed the Atlantic arriving in the United Kingdom on the 11th, and was assigned to No.3 Personnel Reception Centre in Bournemouth, England. He then proceeded to other training squadrons until March 20th 1944, when he was posted to No.434 R.C.A.F. Squadron in Croft, England. On the night of June 16th to the 17th, No.434 Squadron was detailed to take part in a 405 aircraft raid on synthetic oil plants in the Sterkrade/Holten area in Germany. F/O Lummis' aircraft, a Halifax bomber number MZ.297, failed to return from this bombing mission and crashed near Altphen, Holland. All seven of the crew, including F/O Lummis were killed and buried in Plot 13, Row I, Grave 2, Amersfoort (Oud Leusden) General Cemetery, Utrecht, Holland.

Service number: J28211

Medals and Awards: 1939-45 Star, Air Crew Europe Star, France and Germany Star, Defence Medal, the Canadian Volunteer Service Medal and clasp and the War Medal 1939-45.

MACALLISTER, Ronald A. **Trooper**
4th Arm. Brig. **WWII**

Ronald Arthur MacAllister was born in Brownburg on July 16th 1924, son of Arthur Earl and Norma Osborne MacAllister. He resided in Brownburg and attended public school until the age of 16. In 1941, he began employment with Canadian Industries Limited, also in Brownsburg, as an apprentice toolmaker. On April 13th 1943, he enlisted in the Canadian Army in Montreal and was immediately taken on strength with No.4 District Depot. On the 30th, he was sent to No.48 Basic Training Centre in St-Jean, Quebec. He remained there until July 1st, when he was sent to No.1 Canadian Armored Corps Training Centre Reserve in Borden, Ontario for armored training. Ronald left Canada on February 16th 1944, and arrived safely in the United Kingdom on the 24th, and was assigned to No.3 Canadian Armored Corps Reinforcement Unit. He remained with this unit until July 5th, when he was transferred to the 21st Canadian Armored Regiment (The Governor General's Foot Guards) crossing into France on the 22nd. He remained with the G.G.F.G. until November 3rd, when he was transferred to Headquarters, 4th Canadian Armored Brigade. On February 15th 1945, Trooper Ronald Arthur MacAllister died of wounds received in action in Holland. He was buried the next day in the Holland Canadian Division Cemetery. He was later exhumed and reburied in Plot XV, Row E, Grave 12, Groesbeek Canadian War Cemetery, Gelderland, Holland.

Service number: D131689

Medals and Awards: 1939-45 Star, France and Germany Star, the Canadian Volunteer Service Medal and clasp and the War Medal 1939-45.

MACKENZIE, Duncan C. **L.A.C.**
R.C.A.F. **WWII**

LAC/BAC

Duncan Cameron MacKenzie was born in Peterborough, Ontario on January 2nd 1922, son of Reverend James Alexander MacKenzie and Margaret Elizabeth Hay. Reverend McKenzie was the son of Reverend Duncan MacKenzie, Minister of

Religion in Lost River. Duncan's parents had been married in Lachute in 1919. The MacKenzies moved throughout Canada. Duncan Cameron went from Ontario, to Saskatchewan, Quebec and back to Ontario prior to his enlistment. From 1927 to 1934, he attended King Edward School in Saskatoon, Saskatchewan. He then attended High School at City Park Collegiate also in Saskatoon and graduated in 1938. Afterwards, he travelled to Toronto, Ontario and attended the University of Toronto, graduating in 1942 with a B.A. In June 1941, Duncan found himself in Brownsburg, working as a chemist at the C.I.L. ammunition plant until September 1942. On October 29th 1942, while attending the University of Toronto, he enrolled in the 2nd Battalion, Canadian Officer Training Corps as a private. He remained with the C.O.T.C. until November 26th, when he enlisted in the University Air Training Corps, Royal Canadian Air Force. His brother, Ronald, also enlisted in the R.C.A.F., surviving the War. On May 2nd 1943, Duncan was assigned to No.1 Initial Training School also in Toronto until July 25th, when he was transferred to No.23 Elemental Flying Training School in Davidson, Saskatchewan. Duncan was on his way to becoming a pilot. On September 19th, he was transferred to No.17 Service Flying Training School in Souris, Manitoba, in order to continue his training. Sadly, on November 6th 1943, at approximately 1040hrs, L.A.C. MacKenzie was a passenger in an Avro Anson Mark II aircraft. This aircraft had been on cross country training with an instructor and another airman. For an unknown reason, the aircraft crashed in the bush about 59 miles north-north-east of Souris. All three occupants were killed. A Court of Inquiry was convened and the conclusion was inconclusive. Icing may have played a part in the crash. Duncan Cameron MacKenzie was buried in the Lachute Protestant Cemetery.

Service number: U199219

Medals and Awards: Canadian Volunteer Service Medal and the War Medal 1939-45.

MACRAE, Norman **Gunner**
R.C.A. **WWII**

Norman MacRae was born in Wentworth Township on September 8th 1898, son of Donald and Mary Beaton. Norman grew up in the Lost River area. On October 4th 1916, Norman enlisted with the 229th Overseas Battalion, Canadian Expeditionary Force, in Rouleau, Saskatchewan. He remained in Canada until April 17th 1917, when he boarded the troopship S.S. Northland in Halifax disembarking safely in Liverpool, England on the 29th. He was sent to a segregation camp in Bramshott the next day and taken on strength with the 19th Reserve Battalion. On June 20th, he was transferred to the Canadian Engineer Training Depot in Crowborough. On July 2nd 1918, he was transferred to the 12th Battalion, Canadian Engineers in France. Norman survived the War and left Europe on June 6th 1919. On September 10th 1919, after returning from the War, Norman married Annie McTavish of Harrington, in Montreal. Norman's father, Donald, died in 1927 and his wife Annie died in 1934. At some point, Norman started employment with the Canadian Refractories Ltd company as a miner. By 1940, his son, Grant Alexander, had joined the Canadian Army, surviving the War. Norman enlisted with the Canadian Army on May 31st 1940, in Montreal and was immediately taken on strength by No.4 District Depot. On July 12th, Norman was sent to the Royal Canadian Artillery Training Centre in Petawawa Military Camp, Ontario. On October 28th, Gunner Norman MacRae was found dead. An autopsy revealed that he died of acute alcohol poisoning. Norman was buried in Harrington Shaw's cemetery.

Service number: D9249

Medals and Awards: British War Medal, Victory Medal (1914-1919), Canadian Volunteer Service Medal and the War Medal 1939-45.

MACVICAR, Donald I. **F/Sergeant**
R.C.A.F. **WWII**

LAC/BAC

Donald Irwin McVicar was born in Lachute on July 23rd 1923, son of Amos Nichol and Nettie May Kettle. From 1928 to 1935, Donald attended Primary school in Granby, Quebec and High School in Lachine, Quebec from 1935 to 1941. While in school, Donald enrolled in the Cadet Corps. After High School, he became employed with the Bell Telephone Company in Montreal as a splicer. On September 7th 1942, he enrolled in the Royal Canadian Air Force in Montreal and was assigned to No.5 Manning Depot on the 23rd. He spent some months training and was eventually sent to No.3 Bombing and Gunnery School in MacDonald, Manitoba on June 13th 1943. On September 13th, a year after joining the R.C.A.F., he boarded a troopship and left Canada for the United Kingdom. He arrived safely on the 19th, and was posted the next day to No.3 Personnel Reception Centre in Bournemouth, England. He was assigned to an Operational Training Unit and finally reached his squadron, the 576th, in Elsham Wolds, England on May 14th 1944. On the night of July 28th to the 29th 1944, F/Sgt MacVicar was part of a crew of a Lancaster bomber serial LL905, taking part in a 494 bomber raid on the German city of Stuttgart. On their way back, the bombers were attacked by German night fighters and 39 of the bombers were shot down, including F/Sgt MacVicar's aircraft. His Lancaster crashed near Sarrewerden, Alsace-Lorraine, France. Four of the crew members were killed, including F/Sgt MacVicar, while three were taken prisoner. F/Sgt Donald Irwin MacVicar was buried in a collective grave, along with two of his crew members, in the Sarrewerden Communal Cemetery, Bas-Rhin, France.

Service number: R189676

Medals and Awards: 1939-45 Star, France and Germany Star, Defence Medal, the Canadian Volunteer Service Medal and clasp and the War Medal 1939-45.

MADDEN, Foster **Private**
60th Bn **WWI**

Foster Madden was born in Arundel on November 9th 1895, son of James, a farmer, and Olive Boyd. Foster's father died in 1911, and his mother remarried with William Peter Mott, a farmer from Brownsburg. On August 28th 1915, Foster attested into "B" Company, 60th Battalion of the C.E.F. At that time he listed his trade as being a paving cutter. He remained in Canada until November 6th, when he boarded the troopship S.S. Scandinavian en route to England and the Germans. His troopship docked safely on the 16th, and proceeded to Bramshott with his Battalion. He spent Christmas in England and left for France on February 20th 1916, disembarking in Le Havre. On September 16th, while in the front lines in the area of Courcelette, France, he was reported missing in action. The record keepers annotated his file, on December 5th 1917, that he was no longer listed as missing in action but having been killed on September 16th 1916. He was buried in Plot III, Row G, Grave 20, Courcelette British Cemetery, Somme, France.

Service number: 458570

Medals and Awards: British War Medal and Victory Medal (1914-1919)

MAXWELL, William H. **Sergeant**
R.C.A.F. **WWII**

LAC/BAC

William Harold McQueen Maxwell was born in St-Andrews East on February 12th 1921, son of Arnold Samuel and Isobel Simpson Stephen. He attended St-Andrews East Consolidated School from 1928 to 1938 then Lachute High School for one year. After school, in 1939, he became employed by T. McOuat in Lachute, as a machinist. On December 2nd 1941, he enlisted with the Royal Canadian Air Force, aspiring to become a pilot. He was immediately assigned to No.1 Manning Depot in Toronto, Ontario. On December 22nd, he was sent to No.1 Training Centre also in Toronto. His training continued. On March 15th 1942, he was sent to No.6 Initial Training School which was also located in Toronto. He was sent to No.2 Air Observer School in Edmonton, Alberta, on June 7th. William was promoted to sergeant on September 25th 1942. On October 28th, he boarded a troopship bound for the United Kingdom which he reached safely on November 4th. On the 5th, he was assigned to No.3 Personnel Reception Centre in Bournemouth, England and remained with this Unit for about one month. When he was transferred to No.10 Advanced Flying Unit. On January 2nd 1943, Sgt Maxwell was reported missing after the Anson twin engine aircraft he was the navigator in, was lost off the coast of Scotland. His body was never found. Sgt William Harold McQueen Maxwell is commemorated on Panel 186, Runnymede Memorial, Surrey, United Kingdom.

Service number: R141701

Medals and Awards: Defence Medal, the Canadian Volunteer Service Medal and clasp and the War Medal 1939-45.

MAY, Hector B. **Corporal**
R.H.R. **WWII**

Hector Baillie May was born in Montreal on September 14th 1914, son of James, a molder, and Gertrude Lillian Newton. He was educated in Montreal, attending Sir George Williams Business College for two years after attending High School. In 1930, he began employment with the Dominion Textile Company in Montreal as an office clerk. He remained at their employ until his enlistment. In June 1940, he joined the 2nd Battalion, The Black Watch (Royal Highland Regiment) of Canada, a Reserve unit out of Montreal. Two of his brothers, James Leslie and John also enlisted in the Canadian Army. James Leslie had served with the 5th Canadian Armoured Division and survived the War while John was killed in action in February 1944. On February 12th 1942, Hector enlisted with the Canadian Regular Army in Montreal and was assigned to the Royal Rifles of Canada, promoted to Corporal and sent to Quebec City on the 16th. By August 1942, Cpl May's family had moved from Montreal to Arundel. Hector remained in Canada until May 13th 1943, when he boarded a troopship and crossed the Atlantic Ocean, arriving safely in the United Kingdom on the 22nd, and was assigned to No.5 Canadian Infantry Reinforcement Unit at Tourney Barracks, Aldershot, England for further training and assignment. On August 6th, he was transferred to "A" Company, 1st Battalion, The Black Watch (Royal Highland Regiment) of Canada. He attended courses with Canadian Training School and No.1 Officers Cadet Training Unit until January 14th 1944, when he was returned to the Black Watch. Cpl May landed in France on July 6th. On July 25th 1944, The Black Watch (Royal Highland Regiment) of Canada took part in a disastrous attack at May-Sur-Orne, France. It was during this attack that Cpl Hector Baillie May was killed in action. He was temporarily buried in Plot 2, Row 3, Grave 11 in the Saint-Martin-de-Fontenay Cemetery on August 14th. He was later exhumed and re-burried in Plot III, Row D, Grave 13, Bretteville-Sur-Laize Canadian War Cemetery, Calvados, France.

Service number: E52733

Medals and Awards: 1939-45 Star, France and Germany Star, Defence Medal, the Canadian Volunteer Service Medal and clasp and the War Medal 1939-45.

MAY, John N. **Corporal**
H. & P.E. Regt **WWII**

John Newton May was born in Montreal, on March 30th 1913, son of James, a moulder and Gertrude

Lillian Newton. He attended school in Montreal and left at the age of 16. In 1929, he began employment with the Canadian Car and Foundry Company in Montreal, as a purchasing clerk. He remained with them for 13 years, up to his enlistment in the Army. In July 1940, he joined the 2nd Battalion, The Black Watch (Royal Highland Regiment) of Canada, a Reserve unit out of Montreal. Two of his brothers, James Leslie and Hector Baillie also enlisted in the Canadian Army. James Leslie had served with the 5th Canadian Armoured Division and survived the War while Hector was killed in action in July 1944. On February 10th 1942, two days before his brother Hector enlisted, he attested into the Canadian Regular Army in Montreal and was assigned to the Royal Regiment of Canada on the 16th, and sent to Quebec City. On July 23rd 1942, he was promoted to Corporal while he was stationed in Nanaimo, British Columbia. By August 1942, Cpl May's family had moved from Montreal to Arundel. He remained in British Columbia until he was ready to be shipped overseas. On January 6th 1943, he was sent to Debert, Nova Scotia, awaiting his transport to Europe. On February 4th, he boarded a troopship and sailed for the United Kingdom, arriving safely on the 13th, being sent to No.5 Canadian Infantry Reinforcement Unit at Tourney Barracks, Aldershot, England, the next day. On May 13th, he was transferred to the Hastings and Prince Edward Regiment. On June 29th, he boarded a ship and made the perilous voyage to the Mediterranean Theatre of War and arrived safely in Italy on July 11th. On February 3rd 1944, Cpl John Newton May was killed in the vicinity of Villa Grande, Italy. He was temporarily buried in an improvised cemetery in Ortona and on August 17th, was exhumed and re-interred in Plot VII, Row G, Grave 4, Moro River Canadian War Cemetery, Italy.

Service number: E52727

Medals and Awards: 1939-45 Star, Italy Star, the Canadian Volunteer Service Medal and clasp and the War Medal 1939-45.

McCallister, George W. 2nd Lieutenant
R.A.F. WWI

George Wesley McAllister was born on January 20th 1898, in Compton Township, Quebec, son of George, a farmer and Sarah Delacourt. By 1911, the family had moved to the Brownsburg area of Chatham Township. George's older brother, Gordon William, enlisted with the 92nd Overseas Battalion, C.E.F., on August 20th 1915, in Toronto, Ontario. Gordon survived the War and returned to Ontario afterwards. George crossed to England and joined the Royal Flying Corps and was commissioned a 2nd/Lieutenant on March 10th 1918. On April 25th, he reported to No.2 Training Depot Station, Gullane, Scotland to begin his training as a pilot. Sadly, on August 12th, while at the controls of a Sopwith Camel aircraft number C8329, he failed to recover from a right side spin and crashed, killing him instantly. He was buried in Plot K, Grave 902, Edinburgh Comely Bank Cemetery, Edinburgh, Scotland.

Service number: 2/Lieutenant

Medals and Awards: British War Medal

McCALLUM, Douglas H. Major
R.C.E. WWII

Douglas Harvey McCallum was born in Carberry, Manitoba on October 21st 1909, son of Fergus and Daisy Evelyn Harvey. By 1944, his father was deceased and his mother had re-married and was residing in Lachute. Douglas spent the first three years of his life in Manitoba, then the family moved to Ontario and finally to Quebec. He was educated in Ontario, graduating from the Vankleek Hill Collegiate Institute in 1926 and then enrolling with the International Correspondence School in mechanical engineering, graduating in 1929. He began employment in 1926 with the Canadian International Paper Company in Hawkesbury, Ontario as a chemical tester in a research laboratory. In 1929, he changed jobs and was then employed by the Canadian Ingersoll Rand Ltd Company in Sherbrooke, Quebec in the production and design of portable compressors. He remained with them until December 1929, when he started employment with Darling Brothers Ltd in Montreal, and a few years later in Ottawa as a sales engineer. On December 1st 1937, he enlisted with the 3rd Field Company, Royal Canadian Engineers, an active militia unit in Ottawa, and was commissioned as a 2nd Lieutenant. On September 4th 1939, he attested in the Canadian Active Service Force in Ottawa with the 3rd Company, was now a Lieutenant and assigned as a section commander. His stay in Canada would be short since, on November 24th 1939, he boarded a troopship in Montreal and disembarked in Liverpool, England on December 1st. Douglas remained in England, was promoted to Captain on August 13th 1940, and transferred to the 1st Battalion, Royal Canadian Engineers on September 1st 1941. He remained with the 1st until August 10th 1942, when he was transferred to the 2nd Battalion, Royal Canadian Engineers and promoted to Major. On May 15th 1943, he was once again transferred to another engineer unit, the 31st Field Company, as its Commanding Officer. On July 7th 1944, Major McCallum and his unit landed in France. He was a steadfast and courageous officer as this citation, dated July 23rd, for a Distinguished Service Order recommendation, speaks volume to:

> *"During the night 18-19 July 1944, 2 Canadian Corps made an assault crossing of the River Orne. This operation was one of the most important of the entire campaign, and its failure would have had a serious effect on the whole operation in Normandy. As part of the Corps plan, 31 Canadian Field Company, the Corps of Royal Canadian Engineers, had the task of constructing a bridge over the River Orne at Caen to allow the passage of the so necessary supporting arms. Failure, therefore, to complete construction of this bridge would have had serious effects on the army plan. Major McCallum was in command of this operation and though harassed by mortar and sniper fire and by enemy planes, carried on with the task and brought it to a very successful conclusion. His courage and ability were of the highest order and undoubtedly contributed to the success of the operation."*

Sadly, two days later, on July 25th 1944, Major Douglas Harvey McCallum was killed in the vicinity of Cormelles, France. He was temporarily buried in Caen, on the 27th, and later exhumed and reburied in Plot XI, Row F, Grave 5, Bretteville-sur-Laize Canadian War Cemetery, Calvados, France.

Service number: Major

Medals and Awards: Companion of the Distinguished Service Order (DSO), 1939-45 Star, France and Germany Star, Defence Medal, The Canadian Volunteer Service Medal and clasp and the War Medal 1939-45.

McCALLUM, Rupert **Corporal**
2ND Bn **WWI**

Rupert McCallum was born in Lachute, on January 15th 1882, the son of Alexander, a blacksmith, and Maria Bain. His mother died when he was only four years old and he remained with his father in Lachute until 1901. On January 25th 1902, he enlisted with the 2nd Imperial Light Horse in Port-Elizabeth, South Africa. At that time, Britain was still at war with the Boer Republics (2nd Boer War). He was discharged from further service due to the ending of hostilities on June 30th 1902. Following his discharge from the Imperial Light Horse, he enlisted with the Cape Mounted Riflemen on July 15th, in Cape Town, South Africa. While serving in South Africa, his father, Alexander, died in 1910 in Lachute. Rupert returned to Canada on March 21st 1914, when he landed in Halifax on board the ship S.S. Alsatian. He had been away from Canada for 12 years! Five months after his arrival, the world witnessed the start of World War One and Rupert wouldn't be left out of it. On September 22nd 1914, he travelled to Valcartier and promptly enlisted with the Divisional Headquarters Subordinate Staff, 1st Division, C.E.F., as a batman. His stay in Canada was short lived. He was part of the 56 other ranks who boarded the R.M.S. Franconia and left Canada bound for England and the War on October 3rd, landing in Plymouth, England, 12 days later. The entire Canadian Division proceeded to Salisbury Plains for training. He remained in England for several months, getting into trouble on a few occasions for being absent without leave. On April 26th 1915, he joined his newly appointed unit, the 2nd Battalion in the Fields of Flanders. He was promoted to Lance Corporal on May 16th, and again to the rank of Corporal on May 6th, 1916. On June 4th 1916, Cpl Rupert McCallum was killed by artillery fire, while in the trenches, east of Zillebeke, Belgium. He is commemorated on the Ypres (Menin Gate) Memorial, West-Vlaanderen, Belgium.

Service numbers: 1247 (Imperial Light Horse), 3914 (Cape Mounted Riflemen), 1877 (2nd Battalion)

Medals and Awards: Queen's South Africa Medal with Transvaal and Orange Free State clasps, 1914-1915 Star, British War Medal and Victory Medal (1914-1919)

McGIBBON, Alex N. — Private
47th Bn — WWI

Alexander Norman McGibbon was born in Chatham Township on June 13th 1890, the son of William Daniel and Mary Lothian. Both his parents died in 1896, leaving him and his sibblings orphans. By 1901, he was residing with the McKenzie family in Chatham Township. In 1915, he was residing in British Columbia. He enlisted with "A" Company of the 11th Canadian Mounted Rifles in Vancouver, British Columbia on March 27th 1915. At that time he was single and a farmer. He remained in Canada until he boarded the troopship S.S. Lapland on July 8th 1916, arriving safely in England on the 25th. Pte McGibbon remained in England and suffered an injury to his knee on August 9th, requiring hospitalization. Once his injury healed, he transferred to the 24th Reserve Battalion, in Bramshott, on January 13th 1917. He remained with the 24th until March 5th, when he was transferred to the 47th Battalion. He would join his new unit in the fields of battle three days later. His injuries continued. While in the field, he again injured his knee in April, and then in May he was wounded by gunshot to his right arm and back. He was evacuated back to England until October 4th, when he returned to the 47th. On January 5th 1918, while in trenches in the area of Arras, France, he was severely wounded by shrapnel to his leg and hand, causing fractures to his tibia and fibula. He didn't survive these wound. He died that same day at No.42 Casualty Clearing Station. He was buried in Plot III, Row C, Grave 11, Aubigny Communal Cemetery Extension, Pas-de-Calais, France.

Service number: 116227

Medals and Awards: British War Medal and Victory Medal (1914-1919)

McINTOSH, George **CQMS**
60th Bn **WWI**

George McIntosh was born in Aberdeen, Scotland on February 5th 1887, son of William, a warehouse porter, and Mary Ann Gray. On February 5th 1904, he joined the Royal Navy as a signalman on the training ship H.M.S. Caledonia. He served on other training and warships until he left the R.N. on August 29th 1907. He immigrated to Canada sometime before 1915. On the 14th of June 1915, he enlisted with "D" Company, 60th Battalion, C.E.F., in Montreal. On November 6th, he embarked on the troopship S.S. Scandinavian in Montreal en route to England and arrived safely on the 16th. Pte McIntosh was promoted to

Corporal on December 3rd, but was demoted on January 14th 1916, for causing a disturbance. He remained in England until February 21st, when he landed in Le Havre, France with his Battalion. In June, he took a signaling course with the Royal Flying Corps. On August 31st, he fell ill with tonsillitis and influenza and was sent to a Casualty Clearing Station for treatment. On October 3rd, he was sent back to England, where he remained, until he was transferred to the 4th Battalion, Canadian Railway Troops on February 9th 1917, returning to France five days later. On September 25th, he was again promoted to Corporal and again, on January 21st 1918, he was promoted to C.Q.M.S. He remained in France and on November 11th, the War came to an end. He was granted a 14 day leave period in England on December 13th. It was while on leave in England, that he fell seriously ill with influenza. On December 23rd, he was admitted to the Canadian Military Hospital in Witley, England where he was treated and eventually released. But C.Q.M.S. McIntosh's influenza returned and he was re-admitted to No.12 Canadian General Hospital in Bramshott on February 19th 1919, where he was listed as seriously ill. He was again treated and discharged from the hospital on March 7th. He left Southampton, England to return home on board the troopship S.S. Aquitania on May 18th, and arrived in Halifax, Nova Scotia on the 25th. From Halifax, he proceeded to Montreal where, on May 27th, almost four years since his enlistment, he was demobilized and left the Army. George went to work as a telegraphist and on August 5th, he married, in Montreal, Maggie Evelyn Shaw of Lachute. The couple eventually moved to Lachute. Sadly, George became ill again and had to be admitted to the sanatorium in Ste-Agathe, where, on September 13th 1923, he died. The death was directly attributed to his military service. He was buried two days later, in the Lachute Protestant cemetery.

Service number: 457357

Medals and Awards: British War Medal and Victory Medal (1914-1919)

McKercher, Peter **Private**
73rd Bn **WWI**

Short history 73rd Battalion

Peter McKercher was born in Kenyon Twp, Glengarry County, Ontario on February 13th 1895, son of Donald, a farmer and Janet McLean. He remained in Kenyon Twp and began working with the Bank of Ottawa, Maxville Branch, on April 10th 1913. He transferred to the Grenville Branch on February 28th 1914 and to the Lachute Branch on August 31st. On September 15th 1915, he enlisted with No.13 Platoon, "D" Company, 73rd Battalion, C.E.F., in Montreal. He remained in Canada until March 31st 1916, when he and his Battalion boarded the troopship S.S. Adriatic in Halifax, bound for England and the German Armies. They arrived safely in Liverpool on April 9th, and proceeded to Bramshott. On August 12th, he embarked for Le Havre, France and the lines of the Western Front. He was transferred to the 42nd Battalion on April 19th 1917. On June 15th, he suffered a slight wound to his right leg and evacuated from the front lines. From there, he was sent to No.20 General Hospital in Camiers, France for further treatment and finally discharged from the hospital on August 1st. He eventually rejoined his Battalion on October 15th.

Pte McKercher, as thousands of other Canadian soldiers, became ill with bronchitis and tuberculosis and had to be admitted to No.12 Canadian Field Hospital on January 7th 1918. His fight with the disease was just beginning. He remained in hospitals in England until he was repatriated to Canada. He arrived in Halifax on May 15th, on board the H.M.H.S. Llandovery Castle. He made his way to Montreal and was admitted to Drummond Military Convalescent Hospital on the 18th. He was discharged from the Army on July 31st 1918, having been found medically unfit for further service. Peter never recovered and died on February 23rd 1919, at his father's residence in Maxville, Ontario. He was buried in the Maxville cemetery.

Service number: 132500

Medals and Awards: British War Medal and Victory Medal (1914-1919)

McOUAT, George M. G.G.F.G. **Guardsman WWII**

George Mervyn McOuat was born in Lachute on September 12th 1914, son of Duncan, a farmer in the parish of St-Jerusalem and Ida Ellen Walker. George's mother passed away in 1927. He attended school, completing his grade eight. George enlisted with the Royal Montreal Regiment on June 10th 1940, in Westmount, Quebec. At that time, he reported residing at 19 Bethany Street in Lachute and was a driver by trade. His older brother Laurence would also enlist as a Gunner in the Canadian Army and survived the War. George remained in Canada until August 24th 1940, when he departed Halifax en route to the United Kingdom and World War II. He arrived safely and landed in Gourock,

Scotland on September 5th, and was assigned to No.1 Signals Holding Unit on November 14th, in Aldershot, England. He remained in England for a few years, attending numerous courses and training. On June 18th 1943, he was transferred to No. 32 Reconnaissance Regiment and later, on March 19th 1944, he was transferred to the 21st Canadian Armored Regiment (Governor General's Foot Guards). He crossed the Channel and landed in France on July 23rd. On the night of March 26th 1945, while in the Reichwald area in Germany, Gdmn McOuat was killed instantly when an enemy artillery shell landed in his slit trench. He was buried in Bedburg, Germany temporarily. He was later exhumed and reburied in Plot XI, Row B, Grave 11 Groesbeek Canadian War Cemetery, Gelderland, Holland.

Service Number: D77332

Medals and Awards: 1939-45 Star, France and Germany Star, Defence Medal, the Canadian Volunteer Service Medal and clasp and the War Medal 1939-45.

McVICAR, Alexander **Private**
46th Bn **WWI**

Alexander McVicar was born in Harrington Township on March 30th 1898, son of Walter and Jane Fraser. His mother Jane died one week later on April 7th. Alexander enlisted with the 210th Overseas Battalion, C.E.F., on May 27th 1916, in Moose Jaw, Saskatchewan. At the time of his enlistment, he was a farmer and residing in Marquis, Saskatchewan. He left Canada on the troopship H.M.T. Carpathia on April 9th 1917, and arrived in Liverpool, England on the 22nd. Immediately upon arrival, he was transferred to the 19th Reserve Battalion, and proceeded to

Bramshott. On June 16th, he was again transferred, this time to the 46th Battalion, joining his new Battalion in the field eight days later. On August 21st 1917, at 0435hrs, the 46th Battalion attacked in the vicinity of Lievin, France. After the day's action, Pte McVicar was nowhere to be found and was reported missing. In fact, Alexander had been captured by the Germans and had been held as a prisoner of war. Pte Alexander McVicar died on or since the 4th of November 1917 at Feldlazarette (German Military Hospital), Le Forest and was buried in Grave 168, Le Forest Communal Cemetery, France. He was later exhumed and reinterred in Plot VI, Row H, Grave 19, Cabaret-Rouge British Cemetery, Souchez, Pas-de-Calais, France.

Service number: 255640

Medals and Awards: British War Medal and Victory Medal (1914-1919)

MCVICAR, Walter H. **Private**
H.L.I. of C. **WWII**

Courtesy The Watchman

Walter Henry McVicar was born in Rivington on January 2nd 1924, son of Victor, a merchant and Laura Jane Trineer. Victor had enlisted with the Canadian Expeditionary Force during WWI. Walter Henry remained with his family in Rivington his entire young life. He attended primary and secondary schools in Hawkesbury, leaving at 17 years old. In 1940, he began working for Canadian Refractories Limited in Kilmar, Quebec as a screen analyst in a chemistry laboratory. He enlisted with the

Canadian Army on July 22nd 1941, in Montreal. He was sent to Debert, Nova Scotia and joined up with the 17th Duke of York Royal Canadian Hussars, an armoured unit, five days later. On August 19th, he was resent to Montreal and taken on strength with No.4 District Depot. No doubt the 17th had learned that Trooper McVicar was only 17 years old and as such sent him back to Montreal. He remained with this unit until February 13th 1943, when he was sent to No.41 Basic Training Centre in Huntingdon, Quebec. On April 13th, after basic training, he was sent to No.A27 Reconnaissance Training Centre in Dundurn, Saskatchewan. He remained in Canada until October 20th, when he boarded a troopship and left, enroute to the United Kingdom. He reached the U.K. safely and disembarked on October 30th, and was posted to No.1 Canadian Armored Corps Reinforcement Unit. On July 23rd 1944, he was re-assigned to No.2 Canadian Armored Corps Reinforcement Unit until October 6th, when, he was transferred to the Highland Light Infantry of Canada. Four days later, Pte McVicar and his Regiment landed in France. World War II was still raging and fierce fighting lay ahead. On November 1st, Pte McVicar was wounded in action. He was evacuated and sent to No.12 Canadian General Hospital for treatment. He was returned to his Regiment on the 11th. As if one wound received in battle wasn't enough, on December 27th, he was, once again, wounded in action while in Holland. He had been hit by shrapnel from a high explosive shell in the right lumbar and upper chest. He was evacuated to No.5 Field Dressing Station. This time he would not survive. Sadly, on January 8th 1945, Pte Walter Henry McVicar died of his wounds. He had just turned 21. On January 10th, he was buried in Plot I, Row 4, Grave 1, Nijmegen Canadian Military Cemetery, Holland. He was later exhumed and reburied in Plot I, Row F, Grave 14,

Groesbeek Canadian War Cemetery, Gelderland, Holland.

Service Number: D3995

Medals and Awards: 1939-45 Star, France and Germany Star, Defence Medal, the Canadian Volunteer Service Medal and clasp and the War Medal 1939-45.

MENZIES, John **Driver**
10th C.F.A. **WWI**

John Stevens Menzies was born in Lachute on February 10th 1894, son of John Basil, a medical doctor and Hattie Maria Stevens. Dr Menzies came to Lachute from Lanark County, Ontario in 1887 and was a respected physician. He had graduated from McGill University in 1879. John Stevens' paternal grandfather had been Lanark County's Registrar. Dr Menzies died in 1912. John Stevens remained in Lachute until he enlisted with the 79th Battery, C.E.F., on May 22nd 1917, in Montreal. He remained in Canada until he boarded the troopship H.M.T. Megantic on November 19th, and crossed the Atlantic to land in Liverpool, England on December 7th. On his arrival, he proceeded to Whitley and on the 8th was transferred to the Reserve Brigade, Canadian Field Artillery. He remained in England for several months, until April 18th 1918, when he crossed the Channel and landed in France where he proceeded to the C.C.R.C. On July 16th, he was posted to the 10th Brigade, Canadian Field Artillery. On September 6th 1918, while in the Arras sector, Driver John Stevens Menzies was wounded and died on the same day at No.9 Canadian Field Ambulance. He was buried in Plot II, Row C, Grave 38, Vis-en-Artois British Cemetery, Haucourt, Pas-de-Calais, France.

Service number: 1251951

Medals and Awards: British War Medal and Victory Medal (1914-1919)

MILLER, Hugh **L/Corporal**
R.H.R. **WWII**

Hugh Quinton Miller was born in Montreal on October 1st 1912, son of Quinton, a clerk of the city of Montreal and Martha Jane Simms. He attended public school in Rosemount, Quebec and left at the age of 14. From 1927 to 1928, he was employed as a labourer in the shipping department at Eaton's; from 1928 to 1938 as an assembler for the Marconi Radio Company and from 1938 until he enlisted, as an inspector in the bottling department for 7-Up Company. Hugh married Francis Downey in Arundel on November 26th 1933. On July 1st 1940, Hugh enlisted in the Canadian Army in Montreal and was immediately taken on strength with the 1st Battalion, The Black Watch (Royal Highland Regiment) of Canada in Montreal. On July 25th, he was sent to the Canadian Infantry Training Centre in Aldershot, Nova Scotia. He remained in Canada until February 16th 1941, when he boarded a troopship in Halifax, crossed the Atlantic and landed safely in Gourock, Scotland on March 1st. On disembarking, he was assigned to No.2 Canadian Infantry Holding Unit in Witley, England until May 15th, when he was assigned to the 1st Battalion, R.H.R. On August 19th 1942, Operation Jubilee, the raid on the port city of Dieppe, France, began. The armada of ships crossed the English Channel and the Canadian troops, which included the 1st Battalion R.H.R., disembarked. The fighting was deadly and the Canadian casualties mounted. Hundreds of troops could not get off the beach and eventually the order to return to the landing ships was given. The raid was a disaster. Pte Miller was one of the lucky ones, managing to return safely to England the next day. He remained in the United Kingdom training and attending courses. On February 24th 1944, L/Cpl Miller was involved in a motorcycle accident in the Horsham (England) area and suffered serious injuries to his right leg. He was taken to No.9 Canadian General Hospital for treatment. A Court of Inquiry was convened on March 2nd, and exonerated L/Cpl Miller of any negligence or fault in the accident. Following his stay at the hospital, he was sent back to Canada and was admitted to Ste-Anne's Hospital in Montreal on April 14th. His military service was over. On June 6th 1944, the same day the Allied Armies were invading Normandy, L/Cpl Miller was discharged from the Army in Montreal, having been found unable to meet the required military standards. Hugh Miller, having been discharged from Ste-Anne's Hospital, proceeded to Lost River. It was during a visit to Lost River that he was fatally shot. The Sûreté du Quebec police force investigated and accused a Lost River resident who was later acquitted of manslaughter charges. L/Cpl Miller was buried in the Arundel (Protestant) cemetery.

Service Number: D82462

Medals and Awards: 1939-45 Star, Defence Medal, the Canadian Volunteer Service Medal and clasp and the War Medal 1939-45.

MILLER, William R. **Lieutenant**
R.C.E. **WWII**

William Robert Miller was born in Lachute on March 26th 1916, son of Robert and Louisa Beech. Robert attended school, graduating from the

Lachute High School in 1934. From 1934 to 1940, he was employed as a salesman with the Cottingham Supply Company of Lachute. On July 6th 1940, he married Hazel Nellie Tibbits in Montreal, Quebec. William Robert enlisted in the Canadian Army on June 28th 1940, in Montreal and was taken on strength with No.4 District Depot until July 17th, when he was transferred to No.2 Canadian Pioneer Battalion, Royal Canadian Engineers at Camp Borden, Ontario. He remained in Canada until August 22nd, when he boarded a troopship in Halifax, Nova Scotia, enroute for the United Kingdom, disembarking safely in Gourock, Scotland on September 4th. On the 16th, he was promoted to Corporal and stationed in Bordon, England. On September 17th 1942, hHe was again promoted, this time to Lance Sergeant on. Sgt Miller was commissioned on October 16th 1943, promoted to Lieutenant and assigned to the Engineers Reinforcement Unit. Lieut. Miller boarded a troopship on November 14th, and sailed to the Mediterranean Theater of Operations, reaching Italy safely on the 27th. Once in Italy, he was posted to No.4 Field Park Squadron and, on March 15th 1944, to No.10 Field Squadron, Royal Canadian Engineers until January 16th 1945, when he returned to No.4 Field Park Squadron. He remained in Italy until February 21st, when he was transported to France, arriving safely two days later. He returned to the United Kingdom on March 8th, being assigned to No.1 Canadian Engineers Reinforcement Unit. Lieutenant Miller became ill and was admitted to No.17 Canadian General Hospital on April 27th, and transferred to No.11 Canadian General Hospital on May 2nd, diagnosed with pulmonary tuberculosis in his right lung. A medical board was convened and returned a verdict that Lieut. Miller was no longer fit for military duty. As a result, he returned to Canada on June 16th, and was admitted to Ste. Anne de

Bellevue Military Hospital in Montreal on the 19th. His illness worsened, and was discharged from the military on August 14th 1945. On March 9th 1946, he was Mentioned in Despatches in recognition of gallant and distinguished services. Sadly, on June 25th, Lieutenant William Robert Miller died. He was buried on the 28th in the Lachute Protestant Cemetery.

Service Number: Lieutenant

Medals and Awards: Mentioned in Despatches, 1939-45 Star, Italy Star, France and Germany Star, Defence Medal, the Canadian Volunteer Service Medal and clasp and the War Medal 1939-45.

MILLS, Thomas **Private**
19th R.I.R. **WWI**

Thomas Mills was born on February 27th 1881, in Ballygowan, Ireland, son of Thomas, a sett maker and Rebecca Murray Magee. On September 21st 1908, Thomas married Susannah Moore in Downpatrick, County Down, Ireland. Thomas and his wife immigrated to Canada sometime in 1908 and settled in Brownsburg. The Mills had three children born in Brownsburg. Sadly, on September 5th 1914, Susannah died and Thomas and his children returned to Ireland after her death. On July 8th 1916, he enlisted with the 19th Battalion, Royal Irish Rifles in Belfast. At the time of his enlistment he was residing at 37 Delaware Street in Belfast. Thomas never left Ireland and became ill, having contracted tuberculosis. On May 30th 1917, he was discharged from the Army, having been found no longer physically fit for War service. On September 18th 1917, Thomas Mills died at his father's residence in

Belfast. He was buried in the Ballygowan Churchyard on the 20th.

Service number: 19/537

Medals and Awards: None

MONETTE, René **Private**
R22eR **WWII**

René Monette was born in Lachute on March 31st 1919, son of Josephat, an electrician and Eva Paquette. René remained with his family in Lachute throughout his early years. On December 9th 1939, he married Rita Beauséjour in Lachute. On August 13th 1941, he enlisted with the Régiment de Maisonneuve in Montreal and was taken on strength with No.4 District Depot, waiting for his training to begin. On September 17th, he was assigned to No.41 Training Centre in St-Jérôme, Quebec. His stay in St-Jérôme was long. Pte Monette was disciplined on many occasions for being absent without leave and sentenced to detention more than once. This, no doubt, would explain why Pte Monette remained at No.41 Training Centre for so long. On August 6th 1943, he was sent to No.47 Training Centre in Valleyfield, Quebec. On September 7th, he went from Valleyfield to No.1 Transit Camp in Windsor, Nova Scotia, leaving Canada on September 13th, and arrived safely in the United Kingdom on the 19th. On the 20th he reported to No.6 Canadian Infantry Reinforcement Unit at Algonquin Camp, Witley, England. He remained in the United Kingdom until he was sent to the Central Mediterranean Theater of War, landing in Italy on February 18th 1944. On April 4th, he was assigned to the Royal 22e Régiment. On April 23rd 1944, Pte Monette was killed by enemy mortar fire while in the front lines. He was buried in Casa

Berardi near Ortona, Italy. On July 25th, he was exhumed and reburied in plot II, Row 12, Grave 12, Moro River Canadian War Cemetery, Italy.

Service Number: D59206

Medals and Awards: 1939-45 Star, France and Germany Star (this is an error as Pte Monette should have been awarded the Italy Star), Defence Medal, the Canadian Volunteer Service Medal and clasp and the War Medal 1939-45.

MOORE, Edward H. **Private**
1st C.M.R. **WWI**

Edward Harrison Moore was born on April 14th 1892, in Chatham Township, son of Samuel, a farmer and Mary Jane Bigelow. His father died in 1904. Edward Harrison enlisted with the 1st Canadian Mounted Rifles, C.E.F. on December 29th 1914, in Saskatoon, Saskatchewan. This wasn't his first time in the military as he had served three years with the 11th Regiment, Argenteuil Rangers prior to his enlistment. He remained in Canada until June 12th 1915, when he and the 1st C.M.R. boarded the troopship S.S. Megantic and left Montreal for Great-Britain and the War, arriving safely on the 21st. He remained in England until he crossed into France on September 22nd, remaining with his unit. He became ill in the beginning of December with influenza and was treated and finally returned to his duty on December 26th. Again, on March 30th 1916, Pte Moore was sent to the hospital as he had developed an ulcer to his leg. He was treated and rejoined the 1st C.M.R. on May 13th. On June 2nd, the 1st C.M.R., along with other C.E.F. units of the 3rd Division, held the frontline in the area of Maple Copse, Somme, France. At about 0830hrs, the Germans opened up with a heavy artillery bombardment followed by an assault on the Canadian lines. This was the start of the battle of Mount Sorrel. The Battalion held its ground until it could no longer and the remnants retreated to the rear to mount a defence in the next trench line. At the start of the Battle, the 1st C.M.R. fielded 21 officers and 671 other ranks. By the end of the day, 20 officers and 536 other ranks were casualties, an appalling 80% casualty rate. Pte Edward Harrison Moore was part of the casualties on that day having been reported missing. He was never found. He is commemorated on the Ypres (Menin Gate) Memorial, West-Vlaanderen, Belgium.

Service numbers: 106412

Medals and Awards: 1914-1915 Star, British War Medal and Victory Medal (1914-1919)

MOORE, Russell **Private**
28th Bn **WWI**

Russell Mott Moore was born in Chatham Township on September 23rd 1895, son of William John, a farmer, and Jessie Mott. By 1911, Russell was working for the Grand Trunk Railway in the Algoma West District of Ontario. On December 22nd 1914, he enlisted with the 52nd Battalion, C.E.F., in Port Arthur, Ontario. He remained in Canada until he sailed for England on board the S.S. Scandinavian, leaving Montreal on June 17th 1915. He arrived in England safely and proceeded to Shorncliffe, where, for an unknown reason, he re-attested into the 52nd Battalion on July 23rd. On August 8th, he was transferred to the 8th Battalion and was sent to the European mainland, joining his new Battalion in the field. As occurred frequently during the War, he was again transferred to the 28th Battalion on March

21st 1916. On June 7th, while in the trenches, he suffered a gunshot wound to his back and was removed from the front lines and admitted to the Australian Hospital in Wimereux, France. From there, he was evacuated back to England for further treatment and convalescence. He returned to the 28th Battalion on December 6th of the same year. On April 20th 1917, while in the Vimy sector, he was one of three soldiers reported missing. On July 11th, the Canadian Expeditionary Force received correspondence from the International Red Cross advising that, according to German Sources, Pte Russell Moore had died on the 20th of April, while a prisoner of war and had been buried in Grave 1264 of the Henin-Lietard Davey Fosse German cemetery, five miles from Lens, France. He was later exhumed and re-interred in Plot XV, Row L, Grave 37, Cabaret-Rouge British Cemetery, Souchez, Pas-de-Calais, France.

Service numbers: 438480

Medals and Awards: 1914-1915 Star, British War Medal and Victory Medal (1914-1919).

MORGAN, William L. **Private**
1st C.M.R. **WWI**

William Leslie Morgan was born in Weir on October 16th 1895, son of John, a farmer and of Fannie Culquhoun. He remained with his parents until October 12th 1917, when he travelled to Montreal and enlisted with the 249th Battalion, C.E.F. On December 27th, he married Margaret Lloyd of Verdun, Quebec. He remained in Canada until February 18th 1918, when he boarded the troopship H.M.T. Saxonia in Halifax, disembarking in Liverpool, England on March 4th. On his arrival he proceeded to Bramshott and was immediately transferred to the 15th Reserve Battalion. On May 11th, he was transferred to the 1st C.M.R. and joined his Battalion in France. On September 29th 1918, while taking part in an attack North West of Cambrai, Pte William Leslie Morgan was struck by enemy machinegun fire and instantly killed. His Battalion suffered 81 killed and 247 wounded on this day. He was buried in Plot II, Row G, Grave 2, Raillencourt Communal Cemetery Extension, Nord, France.

Service numbers: 1069779

Medals and Awards: British War Medal and Victory Medal (1914-1919).

MORRISON Russel C. **Corporal**
50th Bn **WWI**

Russell Chapman Morrison was born in Brownsburg on March 21st 1893, son of William and Mary Brown McGibbon. By 1916, Russell and his family had moved to Calgary, Alberta and William was working as a merchant. On May 2nd 1916, Russell Chapman enlisted with the 187th Overseas Battalion, C.E.F. in Red Deer, Alberta. At the time of his enlistment, he reported that he was residing on 15th Avenue West in Calgary, was an accountant and had served one year with the 15th Light Horse in Calgary. On May 12th, he was promoted to acting sergeant. He remained in Canada until December 15th, when he boarded the troopship H.M.T. Olympic, reaching England safely on the 26th. He made his way to Witley where, on February 3rd 1917, he was transferred to the 21st Reserve Battalion. On June 25th, he reverted to the rank of private in order to serve with the 50th Battalion on the Front. He landed the next day in Etaples, France and joined the 50th in the field. He was promoted to corporal on

June 21st. On August 23rd 1917, Corporal Russell Chapman Morrison was killed in action in the trenches west of Lens, France. He was buried in Plot I, Row L, Grave 7, Aix-Noulette Communal Cemetery Extension, Pas-de-Calais, France.

Service number: 883052

Medals and Awards: British War Medal and Victory Medal (1914-1919).

MORRISON, William E. **Sergeant**
R.C.A.F. **WWII**

Courtesy The Watchman

William Earl Morrison was born in Arundel on May 8th 1916, son of Alfred Benjamin, a farmer in Arundel and his wife, Florence Chaffey. He was educated in Arundel, attending the Protestant School from 1923 to 1934. From 1938 to 1940, he was enrolled in a correspondence program with Chicago Vocational Training, taking diesel, auto and aero engines. He was employed by several businesses from 1935 to his enlistment in 1940, including Arundel Butter and Cheese, Gordon's Garage, International Paper Company and Pioneer Transportation Company. On August 17th 1940, William Earl enlisted with the Royal Canadian Air Force in Montreal and was sent to No.2 Manning Depot in Brandon, Manitoba. On September 18th, he was sent to the Technical Training School in St-Thomas, Ontario until February 6th 1941, when he was sent to No.5 Bomber Squadron in Dartmouth, Nova-Scotia. William Earl was married to Gula Maud Taylor on June 28th 1941, in West Shefford,

Quebec. On August 29th, he was transferred to No.6 Repair Depot in Trenton, Ontario. It was while posted in Trenton that, on November 24th 1943, at approximately 0015hrs, Sgt William Earl Morrison was riding his bicycle along Highway 2 in Sidney Township and was struck by a transport truck and killed instantly. He was buried in Plot 7, Section F, Arundel (Methodist) Cemetery.

Service Number: R66877

Medals and Awards: War Medal 1939-45 and the Canadian Volunteer Service Medal.

MORROW, Charles E. C.F.C. — **Captain WWI**

Charles Ernest Morrow was born on January 3rd 1873 in Chatham Township, son of John and Elizabeth Jane Morrow. Little is known of him prior to his enlistment in the C.E.F. He enlisted in Strathcona, Alberta on December 20th 1915, with "A" Company of the 151st Overseas Battalion and was residing in Edmonton, Alberta. He had served with "B" Squadron, 6th Hussars as a Captain. On his attestation papers, he listed his sister, Margaret McNish from St-Thomas Ontario, as his next of kin. He remained in Canada until October 3rd 1916, when he boarded the troopship S.S. Californian. His troopship reached England and he landed safely in Liverpool on the 13th. On arrival, he was transferred to the 11th Reserve Battalion in Shorncliffe. On December 20th, he was diagnosed with atonic dyspepsia and at that time, the Medical Officer wrote that he was unfit for general service. This condition lasted until April 5th 1917, when a medical board advised he was now fit for general service. By then, he had been transferred to the Canadian Forestry Corps. Unfortunately, his return to general service was premature. On May 31st 1917, at 1230hrs, he suffered a heart attack and died at No.10 Company, Canadian Forestry Corps Camp, Aviemore, Inverness-shire. He was buried with full military honours on June 4th, in the Rothiemurchus Parish Churchyard, Inverness-shire, Scotland.

Service number: Captain

Medals and Awards: British War Medal

MULLANEY, Thomas **Private**
19th Bn **WWI**

Thomas Mullaney was born in Stockport, England on July 19th 1896. He immigrated to Canada sometime prior to 1915. On August 16th 1915, he enlisted with the 69th Overseas Battalion, C.E.F. in Montreal. He remained in Canada until April 17th 1916 when he boarded the troopship S.S. Scandinavian and crossed the Atlantic to land in England ten days later. On June 7th, he was transferred to the 23rd Battalion in Otterpool Camp. Three weeks later, on June 28th, he was again transferred, to the 19th Battalion and joined his unit in the field the next day. On September 11th 1916, while in the trenches south west of Courcelette, Pte Mullaney was killed in action. His service file states that he was buried in France. The Commonwealth War Graves Commission informs that he has no known grave and was commemorated on the Vimy Memorial, Pas-de-Calais, France. This suggests that his body had been buried at the time of his death and never found afterwards for the purpose of reburial.

Service number: 120426

Medals and Awards: British War Medal and Victory Medal (1914-1919).

MURDOCH, William M. **F/Sergeant**
R.C.A.F. **WWII**

LAC/BAC

William McKenzie Murdoch was born in Brownsburg on December 11th 1921, son of George David and Katherine Louisa McKenzie. William attended Brownsburg Consolidated School from 1929 to 1939 and Lachute High School from 1939 to 1940. In September 1940, he began employment with the Canadian Industries Ltd, Plastics Division in Brownsburg as an office clerk and paymaster. William enlisted with the Royal Canadian Air Force on March 14th 1941, in Montreal. He was immediately taken on strength with No.1 Manning Depot out of Toronto until April 11th, when he was sent to R.C.A.F. Station Trenton, Ontario. On May 28th, he left Trenton and was sent to No.1 Initial Training School in Toronto. On July 4th, he was sent to No.9 Elemental Flying Training School in Ste-Catherines, Ontario. His flight training lasted only two weeks. On July 19th, he was sent back to Trenton and assigned to the Canadian Training School. On September 15th, he left Trenton and proceeded to No.9 Air Observer School in St-Jean, Quebec. On December 21st, after his air observer training, he was sent to No.6 Bombing and Gunnery School in Mountain View, Ontario. On February 1st 1942, his training continued, this time being sent to No.2 Air Navigation School in Pennfield Ridge, New Brunswick. On March 29th, after his training completed, he arrived safely in the United Kingdom and assigned to No.3 Personnel Reception Center in Bournemouth, England until April 24th, when he was sent to No.2 Advance Flying Unit. On September 23rd, he was finally posted to No. 214 Squadron at R.A.F. Stradishall, England. On February 3rd 1943, Sgt Murdoch was a member of a Stirling I bomber number R9197 which was part of a 263 aircraft raid on Hamburg, Germany. This aircraft took off at 1837hrs from R.A.F. Chedburgh, England. While over Germany, the aircraft was attacked by a night fighter and shot down at approximately 2004hrs, at Leusden, 4 kms south-south-east of Amersfoort, Holland. Sgt Murdoch did not survive the crash. He was buried in Plot 13, Row 5, Grave 82, Amersfoot (Oud Leusden) General Cemetery, Utrecht, Holland.

Service Number: R79291

Medals and Awards: 1939-45 Star, Air Crew Europe Star, Defence Medal, The Canadian Volunteer Service Medal and clasp and the War Medal 1939-45.

NEVEU, Ronald **Private**
R.R. of C. **WWII**

Joseph Camille Ronaldo Neveu was born in Brownsburg on March 23rd 1904, son of Joseph and Angélina Desforges. His father died in 1929. By 1939, he was residing in Maple, a community north of Toronto, and was a farmer by trade. On September 9th 1939, he enlisted with the 1st Battalion, Royal Regiment of Canada in Toronto. On February 6th 1940, Ronald married Marianne Wilson also in Toronto. He remained in Canada until June 10th, when he left Halifax, arriving safely in Reykjavik, Iceland on the 16th. He remained in Iceland until October 28th, when Pte

Neveu sailed for the United Kingdom, disembarking on November 3rd. He spent the next year and a half training for the upcoming Operation Jubilee, a raid on the coast of France. On August 19th 1942, Pte Ronald Neveu was part of the landing force on the disastrous raid at the coastal city of Dieppe. After the battle he was listed as missing. His body eventually washed ashore near Boulogne and he was buried in Equihen Plage Communal cemetery. He was later exhumed and reburied in Plot IV, Row B, Grave 3, Calais Canadian War Cemetery, Leubringhen, Pas-de-Calais, France.

Service Number: B66758

Medals and Awards: 1939-45 Star, Defence Medal, The Canadian Volunteer Service Medal and clasp and the War Medal 1939-45.

NICOLL, George C. **Private**
8th Bn **WWI**

George Christie Nicoll was born in Lachute on March 12th 1891, son of Paul and Elizabeth McFarlane. He remained in Lachute for most of his young life having moved to Port-Arthur, Ontario sometime before 1918. He was drafted into "H" Company, 1st Depot Battalion, Manitoba Regiment, C.E.F. on January 3rd 1918, in Port-Arthur. At the time of his enlistment, he reported working as a bushman and residing at the Vendome Hotel, in Port-Arthur. He remained in Canada for only a few months since, on April 19th, he arrived in England having boarded the troopship S.S. Tunisian. Immediately on arrival, he was transferred to the 18th Reserve Battalion. He remained in England and was transferred to the 52nd Battalion on September 5th. Ten days later, he was transferred one last time, this time to the 8th Battalion, which he joined in the fields of France on the same day. On September 27th, the Canadian Corps attacked at Bourlon Wood and began the offensive against the Canal du Nord. Pte Nicoll's Battalion participated in this offensive and it was during this battle that he was reported missing and listed as killed in action two days later. He was buried in Plot II, Row C, Grave 20, Haynecourt British Cemetery, Nord, France.

Service number: 2383321

Medals and Awards: British War Medal and Victory Medal (1914-1919).

NICOLL, Harold M. **Private**
R.R.C. **WWII**

Courtesy The Watchman 1944

Harold Muir Nicoll was born in Lachute on March 16th 1907, son of Paul, a farmer and Elizabeth McFarlane. His older brother George had seen combat during World War One and was killed in action in 1918. His father, Paul, died in 1921 and his mother in 1937. Harold remained with his family, attending school in the Lachute area and completing Grade seven. After school, he went to Huntingdon Quebec to work at T.B. Stark and Son as a farm labourer. On May 19th 1941, Harold enlisted with the 1st Battalion, Victoria Rifles of Canada, a reserve unit, and was sent to No.41 Training Centre in Huntingdon. While at the Training Centre, on July 14th 1941, he attested into the Canadian Active Service Force and continued his training in Huntingdon. His training continued well into 1942 when, on

June 20th, he was transferred to the 2nd Battalion, The Black Watch (Royal Highland Regiment) of Canada, and was sent to Westmount, Quebec. By February 1st 1943, he was stationed in Halifax, Nova Scotia. On May 13th, he boarded a troopship and sailed for the United Kingdom, arriving safely on the 22nd. Immediately on arrival, he was assigned to No.5 Canadian Infantry Reinforcement Unit, Tourney Barracks, Aldershot, England for further training. On July 9th, he was assigned to the 1st Battalion, The Black Watch (Royal Highland Regiment) of Canada. On July 25th 1944, he crossed into France and joined his new unit, the Royal Regiment of Canada. On August 29th 1944, during the Battalion's attack in the Forêt De La Londe area, France, Pte Harold Muir Nicoll was killed in action. On September 3rd, he was buried in a temporary cemetery near the church in the village of La Londe. He was later exhumed and reburied in Plot XVII, Row G, Grave 12, Bretteville-sur-Laize Canadian War Cemetery, Calvados, France.

Service Number: D72226

Medals and Awards: 1939-45 Star, France and Germany Star, Defence Medal, the Canadian Volunteer Service Medal and clasp and the War Medal 1939-45.

NORMAN, William E. **Private**
16th Bn **WWI**

William Ernest Norman was born in Liverpool, England on November 30th 1888, son of Joseph and Elizabeth Norman. He immigrated to Canada, joining his mother Elizabeth, who resided in Brownsburg. On November 11th 1914, William enlisted with the 30th Battalion, C.E.F., in Victoria, British Columbia. At the time of his enlistment he reported that he had previous military service with the 50th Gordon Highlanders and was a steam engineer by trade. On January 30th 1915, he married Matilda Paulina Johnson in Saanich, B.C. Unfortunately the War called and William left for Europe on February 23rd, arriving in England safely and remained in England until April 26th, when he boarded a ship in Southampton and crossed into France. Sometime after his arrival in France, he was assigned to the 16th Battalion in the front lines. On May 19th 1915, he died of wounds he had received participating in an attack at an orchard, north-east of Festubert, France. He was buried in Plot III, Row D, Grave 51, Bethune Town Cemetery, Pas-de-Calais, France.

Service number: 77904

Medals and Awards: 1914-1915 Star, British War Medal and Victory Medal (1914-1919).

NOYES, Thomas R. **L/Corporal**
7th Bn **WWI**

St . Mungo's Centennial

Thomas Robert Noyes was born in Chatham Township on October 6th 1888, son of John Ostrom and Frances Susan Roe. By 1911, Thomas was no longer residing with his family. In 1914, his parents were residing in Naramata, British Columbia. On September 23rd 1914, Thomas enlisted with "H" Company, 7th Battalion, C.E.F. in Valcartier. At the time of his enlistment, he reported being an engineer by trade and had seen prior military service, having served with the 2nd Foot Guards in Ottawa. His younger brother, John Alexander also enlisted with the C.E.F. in 1916 and survived the War. Thomas boarded the troopship R.M.S. Virginian on October 3rd 1914, and reached Devonport Dockyards, England safely on the 16th. Thomas and his Battalion remained in England until February 12th 1915, when they reached St-Nazaire, France. Thomas' War was about to begin. On March 12th, a month after landing in France, he was promoted to Lance Corporal. The 7th reached the trenches of the Western Front. On April 24th 1915, during the ferocious battle now known as the Second Battle of Ypres, battle which saw the Germans use poison gas on a massive scale, L/Cpl Noyes, while in the trenches near St-Julien, Belgium, was hit by shrapnel from an enemy artillery shell and killed instantly. His body was never found. He is commemorated on the Ypres (Menin Gate) Memorial, West Vlaanderen, Belgium.

Service number: 1579 and 17151

Medals and Awards: 1914-1915 Star, British War Medal and Victory Medal (1914-1919).

PAUL, Clarence E. **Private**
8th Bn **WWI**

Clarence Edward Paul was born on February 1st 1898, son of John and Annie Burns of Chatham Township. He remained in Chatham Township until he enlisted with the Mobile Veterinary Section, 4th Canadian Division, C.E.F. on May 18th 1916, in Montreal. He was one of three brothers who enlisted with the military during World War One. Stanley enlisted with the British Expeditionary Force and John with the C.E.F.'s artillery. This wasn't Clarence's first time in the military as he had previous service in the Militia with the 5th Royal Highlanders of Canada. He boarded a troopship and left Canada on June 21st, arriving in England on the 28th. Two days later he was transferred to No.2 Canadian Veterinary Hospital in Shorncliffe. He remained with No.2 until he was transferred to No.1 Canadian Veterinary Hospital on November 27th, and joined this unit in the fields of France two days later. He remained with the Veterinary Hospital until July 11th 1918, date he was transferred to the 5th Battalion. He remained with the 5th for about one month until he was, once again, transferred. This time he was sent to the 8th Battalion on August 16th. On September 3rd, the 8th Battalion was participating in a major offensive in the Cambrai sector and Pte Paul suffered a gunshot wound to his right leg. He was evacuated from the front lines and sent back to England for treatment and convalescence. He survived his wound and the War and was transferred to the 18th Reserve Battalion on February 19th 1919, awaiting his return to Canada and a long awaited demobilization. On June 14th, he finally boarded the troopship H.M.T. Aquitania in Southampton and disembarked in Halifax, Nova Scotia on the 20th. He was discharged from the Army two days later and planned to reside in Lachute. Clarence Paul died on June 3rd 1921, at Ste-Anne-de-Bellevue Hospital of tuberculosis. He was buried on the 7th in the Lachute Protestant Cemetery.

Service number: 516042

Medals and Awards: British War Medal and Victory Medal (1914-1919).

PAUL, Stanley R. **Private**
Middlesex Regt **WWI**

Stanley Randolph Paul was born in January 1895, son of John and Annie Burns of Chatham Township. He was one of three brothers who enlisted for service in the War. Very little is known of this soldier. He enlisted on October 12th 1915, in the British Army with the 1/8th Battalion, Middlesex Regiment. He was discharged on September 10th 1918. Sadly he survived the War but had been exposed to poison gas and as a result, on February 2nd 1920, he died at Brighton Sanatorium in England. His body was returned to Canada and he was buried on February 27th, in the Lachute Protestant cemetery.

Service number: 2016

Medals and Awards: British War Medal and Victory Medal (1914-1919).

PÉLOQUIN, Alexandre J. **Private**
R22eR **Afghanistan**

Courtesy Monique Chevrier

Alexandre Jacques Péloquin was born in Saint-Jerome, Quebec on December 27th 1988, son of Jacques and Monique Chevrier. Alexandre attended primary school at Ecole Bouchard in Brownsburg and completed his high school at the Polyvalente Lavigne in Lachute. He worked at the Videotron store as a clerk and was a member of the Lachute Cadet Corps for four years. Alexandre enlisted in the Canadian Army on October 26th

2007, in Montreal, as an infantryman. On November 4th, he began his training, having been sent to St-Jean, Quebec for his basic. After graduating, he was sent to Canadian Forces Base Valcartier, Quebec on February 29th 2008, and posted to the 3rd Battalion of the Royal 22ième Régiment. On April 1st 2009, he was sent to Kandahar, Afghanistan. It was during this tour of duty, that, on June 8th, while on foot patrol engaged in Operation Constrictor 2, Pte Péloquin was killed by an improvised explosive device near Nakhonay, Panjwai District. On June 20th, Pte Alexandre Jacques Péloquin was buried with full military honours in the Saint-Louis-de-France Cemetery in Brownsburg.

Service number: N69 865 858

Medals and Awards: General Campaign Star – South-West Asia and Sacrifice Medal.

PIBUS, Henry H. **P/Officer**
R.C.A.F. **WWII**

H. H. Pibus, B.A.

Photo courtesy of Bishop's University Archives, Sherbrooke

Henry Hodsmyth Pibus was born in Knowlton Quebec, on February 14th 1914, son of Luther Henry, a merchant and Annabella Matilda Hodsmyth. He attended St-Joseph's Convent and then Knowlton High School, graduating in 1931. Once High School completed, he attended Bishops University and obtained his B.A. in Education in 1935 and became a teacher. Henry started working immediately for the Knowlton School Board and remained at their employ until 1936, when he was transferred to the Lachute High School as the assistant principal. He remained with the Lachute High School until 1940 when he went to the Protestant School Board of Montreal. On the 20th of August 1940, he enlisted in the Royal Canadian Air Force. Henry spent the next year on training at different units in Canada and graduated as an air observer on April 25th 1941, at No.1 Air Navigation School in Rivers, Manitoba. On April 28th, two days after being appointed a Pilot Officer, Henry married Phyllis Alice Muriel Patterson, a nurse, in Montreal. On May 15th, he embarked for the United Kingdom, arriving on the 30th, and was assigned to No.3 Personnel Reception Center in Bournemouth, England. On July 7th, he was assigned to No.13 Operational Training Unit at R.A.F. Bicester. He was finally transferred to No.82 R.A.F. Squadron, at R.A.F. Odiham, on September 11th. On the 14th, the Squadron returned to R.A.F. Bodney and P/O Pibus followed. The Squadron was assigned to attack enemy shipping in the North Sea and the English Channel. On October 21st 1941, P/O Pibus was the navigator on board a Blenheim Mark IV number 6146, which was part of a group of eight bombers assigned to attack enemy ships off the coast of Holland, between Ymuiden and Schweningen. The formation attacked the ships and P/O Pibus' aircraft was attacked by an ME109 German fighter aircraft and was shot down. The aircraft crashed into the sea about five miles from the convoy. There were no survivors. P/O Pibus' body was never found. He is commemorated on Panel 60, Runnymede Memorial, Surrey, United Kingdom.

Service Number: J5086

Medals and Awards: 1939-45 Star, Air Crew Europe Star, the Canadian Volunteer Service Medal and clasp and the War Medal 1939-45.

POULIN, Jules **Corporal**
Rég. Maisonnneuve **WWII**

Joseph Jules Emile Poulin was born in Fassett, Quebec, on November 10th 1914, son of Joseph and Thérèse Quesnel. He resided with his family in Fassett, Thurso and Lachute and attended public school for three years. Before enlisting into the Canadian Army, Jules worked as a lumberman in L'Annonciation, Quebec for one year, and then was employed as a machine operator for Ayers Limited in Lachute. On December 19th 1941, Jules enlisted in the Canadian Army with the Régiment de Maisonneuve. At the time of his enlistment, he was residing with his father on Grace Street in Lachute, his mother having died in 1937. He was immediately assigned to No.4 District Depot in Montreal. On January 10th 1942, he was sent to No.45 Training Centre in Sorel, Quebec for training. His training continued until May 31st, when he boarded a troopship and sailed for the United Kingdom, arriving safely on June 6th. He was taken on strength with the 2nd Division Infantry Reinforcement Unit upon his arrival in the U.K. He remained with this unit until November 13th, when he was transferred to the Régiment de Maisonneuve. Jules remained in England, undergoing intense infantry training. On July 7th 1944, the Régiment de Maisonneuve crossed the English Channel and landed in France. Jules' war was about to begin. He was promoted to Acting Corporal on August 12th. On October 7th 1944, during the Canadian Army's attack on the Scheldt Estuary in Holland, Corporal Poulin was killed in action during the Battalion's advance towards Hoogerheide. He was buried temporarily on the 10th, in Plot 1, Row 1, Grave 14, Ossendrecht Cemetery, Holland. He was later exhumed and buried in Plot 4, Row C,

Grave 1, Bergen-op-Zoom Canadian War Cemetery, Noord-Brabant, Holland.

Service Number: D59358

Medals and Awards: 1939-45 Star, France and Germany Star, Defence Medal, the Canadian Volunteer Service Medal and clasp and the War Medal 1939-45.

PROSSER, Douglas V. **F/Sergeant**
R.C.A.F. **WWII**

Douglas Vary Prosser was born in Brownsburg on September 27th 1917, son of William Vary, a foreman at Canadian Industries Limited in Brownsburg, and Edith King. He was brother to George Alexander, who was also killed in action on July 27th 1941, while serving with 242 Squadron, Royal Air Force. Douglas attended Brownsburg Public School from 1925 to 1935 and then Lachute High School from 1935 to 1936. After High School, he was employed by Canadian Industries Limited in Brownsburg as a toolmaker. He remained at their employ until 1940, when he went to work for Imperial Oil Limited in Montreal as an engineer. In the same year he found himself working for Canadian Car and Foundry, also in Montreal, as a toolmaker. On May 16th 1941, he enlisted with the Royal Canadian Air Force in Montreal. He was immediately taken on strength by No.1 Manning Depot in Toronto until the 29th, when he was sent to No.4 Bombing and Gunnery School, in Fingal, Ontario. He trained at Fingal Station until July 16th, when he was sent to No.1 Initial Training School in Toronto. On January 9th 1942, Douglas finished his training and was now a pilot in the Royal Canadian Air Force. He sailed for the United Kingdom, arriving safely on February 10th 1942 and was assigned to No.3 Personnel Reception Centre in Bournemouth, England. From No.3 P.R.C. he was sent to No.14 Advanced Flying Unit, No.16 Operational Training Unit and finally, on September 16th, he was posted to No.150 R.A.F. Squadron in Kirmington, England. On November 9th 1942, Sgt Prosser was the pilot-in-command of Wellington III bomber number X3310. Eleven of his Squadron's aircrafts had been tasked to bomb targets in Hamburg, Germany. The bomber took off at 1730hrs and was part of a 213 aircraft raid. Early on, the aircrafts encountered very bad weather including clouds, icing and winds not forecasted. Sgt Prosser's aircraft never returned. His body, as well as his crew's, was located in 1951 and the wreckage in 1989. F/Sgt Douglas Vary Prosser was buried in Collective Grave 24, Row H, Plot 1-6, Jonkerbos War Cemetery, Gelderland, Holland.

Service Number: R104801

Medals and Awards: 1939-45 Star, Air Crew Europe Star, Defence Medal, the Canadian Volunteer Service Medal and clasp and the War Medal 1939-45.

PROSSER, George A. **Sergeant**
R.C.A.F. **WWII**

LAC/BAC

George Alexander Prosser was born in Brownsburg on May 26th 1920, son of William Vary, a foreman at Canadian Industries Limited in Brownsburg and Edith King. He was brother to Douglas Vary, who was also killed in action on November 9th 1942, while serving with 150 Squadron, Royal Air Force. George attended Brownsburg Consolidated School from 1927 to 1934, and then Brownsburg and Lachute High Schools from 1934 to 1938. George continued his education after high school, attending Montreal Technical School from 1938 to 1940. He worked for three months, in the summer of 1939, for Canadian Industries Limited in Brownsburg as an assistant in the drafting room. On July 1st 1940, George enlisted with the Royal Canadian Air Force in Montreal and was taken on strength with No.1 Manning Depot in Toronto the next day. On July 22nd, he was sent to No.1 Initial Training School in Toronto in order to begin his pilot's training. He remained there until September 9th, when he was sent to No.4 Elemental Flying Training School in Windsor Mills, Quebec. On November 26th, he was then sent to No.6 Service Flying Training School in Dunnville, Ontario, to further his training. Sgt Prosser graduated as a pilot on February 10th 1941. On March 4th, he left Canada en route for the United Kingdom, arriving safely on the 19th. Once in the United Kingdom, he was assigned to No.59 Operational Training Unit and on May 5th, was posted to No.242 Squadron at R.A.F. Stapleford Tawney, England. On July 27th 1941, Sgt Prosser's Squadron took off from R.A.F. Manston. His mission was to fly Motor Torpedo Boats escort with his Hurricane fighter number Z3563. The M.T.B.'s attacked German torpedo boats and Sgt Prosser and his Squadron became involved in dog fights with German Me-109 fighters off Dunkirk, France. It was during this battle that Sgt Prosser was shot down. His body was never found. He is commemorated on Panel 61, Runnymede Memorial, Surrey, United Kingdom.

Service Number: R56187

Medals and Awards: 1939-45 Star, Air Crew Europe Star, the Canadian Volunteer Service Medal and clasp and the War Medal 1939-45.

READ, William G. **Private**
42nd Bn **WWI**

Short history 73rd Battalion

William George Read was born in Liverpool, England, on July 12th 1892, son of William George and Elizabeth Townsend. His sister, Eliza, married Theodore Hammond of Hill Head, Lachute in 1913. William immigrated to Canada and enlisted with the 73rd Battalion, C.E.F. in Montreal on September 15th 1915. He was assigned to "D" Company No.13 Platoon, the same Platoon as Privates McKercher and Joss. He remained in Canada until he boarded the troopship R.M.S. Adriatic in Halifax on March 31st 1916, proceeding overseas and the War. He landed safely in Liverpool, his place of birth, on April 10th. He remained in England for four months until his Battalion crossed the Channel and landed at Le Havre, France on August 13th. On March 3rd 1917, while in the trenches, his Battalion was shelled by German artillery. Pte Read was wounded by shrapnel to his right ankle and removed from the frontlines. He was evacuated to England one week later. On September 5th, he was transferred to the 20th Reserve Battalion in Shoreham, England. He remained with this Reserve Battalion until he was assigned to the 42nd Battalion on November 14th, arriving in France on the 16th, and reaching his new Battalion on the 21st. Sadly, Pte William George Read died of alcohol poisoning on February 2nd 1918, while the Battalion was in Noeux-Les-Mines, France. He was buried in Plot IV, Row B, Grave 4, Noeux-Les-Mines Communal Cemetery Extension, Pas-de-Calais, France.

Service number: 132505

Medals and Awards: British War Medal and Victory Medal (1914-1919).

REDDICLIFFE, Frederick **Private**
14th Bn **WWI**

Frederick Friend Reddicliffe was born in Cornwall, England on August 25th 1893, son of John and Ann Reddicliffe. He remained in England until he immigrated to Canada, landing in Portland, Maine on April 26th 1912, having crossed the Atlantic on board the Ascania. He enlisted with the 148th Overseas Battalion, C.E.F. on March 15th 1916, in Lachute. He remained in Canada until September 26th, when he and his Battalion, boarded the troopship S.S. Laconia, in Halifax, and began the crossing of the Atlantic en route for England, arriving safely on October 6th, landing in Liverpool. From Liverpool, the Battalion proceeded to Whitley Camp where Pte Reddicliffe remained until he was transferred to the 14th Battalion on December 13th. He arrived in France the next day. Once in France, he joined the 14th in the trenches facing the Germans. He was temporarily assigned to the 2nd Canadian Tunneling Company on February 8th 1917. Frederick became ill and was sent to the hospital for treatment. He returned to the 2nd Tunneling on March 22nd, and remained with this unit until August 6th. On August 20th, he was attached to the 1st Entrenching Battalion to finally return to the 14th on August 28th. On September 20th 1917, while in the vicinity of Cité St-Pierre, he was struck in the abdomen by shrapnel fired by enemy artillery and died. He was buried in Plot III, Row B, Grave 3, Fosse No.10 Communal Cemetery Extension, Sains-En-Gohelle, Pas-de-Calais, France.

Service number: 841803

Medals and Awards: British War Medal and Victory Medal (1914-1919).

RENAUD, John P. **Private**
24th Bn **WWI**

John Phillip Renaud was born in Arundel on August 18th 1898, son of Augustin and Jane Dubeau. He remained with his family, residing in Weir, until he enlisted with "C" Company of the 148th Overseas Battalion, C.E.F., on January 25th 1916, in Montreal. At the time of his enlistment, he stated being a lumberman. He remained in Canada, having attended Camp Valcartier, until he embarked on the S.S. Laconia in Halifax, on September 27th. He crossed the Atlantic with his Battalion, landing in Liverpool, England on October 6th, proceeding to Witley Camp. On

December 14th, he was transferred to the 2nd Entrenching Battalion and joined this unit in France three days later. He remained with this unit until January 22nd 1917, when he was assigned to Headquarters, 1st Canadian Divisional Engineers. On March 8th, he was once again transferred to the 24th Battalion. On April 9th 1917, during the Canadian Corps' attack on Vimy Ridge, Pte Renaud was killed in action. As it occurred way too often, he was only 18 years old. He is commemorated on Panel 3, Column 2, Lichfield Crater Cemetery, Thelus, Pas-de-Calais France.

Service number: 841237

Medals and Awards: British War Medal and Victory Medal (1914-1919).

RHEAUME, Doris A.J. **Sergeant**
R.C.A.F. **WWII**

Joseph Arthur Doris Rhéaume was born in Hawkesbury, Ontario on July 7th 1921, son of Omer, employee of the Canadian International Paper Co. and Maria Simone Daigneault. By 1945, Omer and Maria were residing in St-Jerusalem parish in Lachute. Doris spent his earlier years growing up in Hawkesbury, residing at 183 Main Street East. He attended St-Joseph Academy from 1927 to 1935 and Hawkesbury French High School from 1935 to 1938. After school, he was employed by Arthur Comtois and, afterwards, by L.P. Thériault as a butcher. On June 6th 1940, Doris enlisted as an air crew with the Royal Canadian Air Force, in Ottawa, Ontario. The next day, he was taken on strength with No.1 Manning Depot in Toronto, Ontario. On June 24th, he was sent to No.1 Initial Training School also in Toronto. His training in the R.C.A.F. had started. On July 19th, he was sent to No.1 Wireless School in Montreal, Quebec. He continued to train with different other units until March 2nd 1941, when he crossed the Atlantic and arrived in the United Kingdom. On July 14th, after a few months in training units, he was transferred to 104 Squadron, Royal Air Force at R.A.F. Driffield, England. On August 28th 1941, Sgt Rhéaume was a member of a Wellington bomber, number W5595E. On this night, 104 Squadron was part of a 118 aircraft raid into Germany with a primary target of Duisburg. Sgt Rhéaume's aircraft took off from Driffield at 2340hrs on a bombing mission. The aircraft failed to return. Sgt Rhéaume was listed as missing after air operations. In October 1941, the Air Ministry received information from the International Red Cross Society advising that Sgt Rhéaume had in fact been killed on August 29th 1941, and he was buried in the Prisoner of War camp cemetery in Neuss, Germany. He was later exhumed and reburied in Plot 6, Row B, Grave 18, Rheinberg War Cemetery, Nordrhein-Westfalen, Germany.

Service number: R539443

Medals and Awards: 1939-45 Star, Air Crew Europe Star, the Canadian Volunteer Service Medal and clasp and the War Medal 1939-45.

RICHARDS, Edwin R. **L/Corporal**
24th Bn **WWI**

Courtesy Peter Duncan

Edwin Ricardo Richards was born in London, England on September 6th 1895, son of George Alfred and Isabella Richards. George Alfred was a stage assistant and residing at 20 Blythe Terrace. Edwin and his family immigrated to Canada, arriving in Quebec City on April 2nd 1905, on board the ship Vancouver. By 1914, he was working as a clerk and his father was residing in Brownsburg. On November 10th 1914, he enlisted with "B" Company of the 24th Battalion, C.E.F. in Montreal. According to his attestation papers, he had prior military service with the 3rd Victoria Rifles of Canada. He remained in Canada until May 11th 1915, when he boarded the troopship S.S. Cameronia, which transported him to England, landing safely on the 20th. He remained in England with his Battalion until he crossed into France, landing at Boulogne on September 16th. He was promoted to Lance Corporal on November 1st. L/Cpl Richards remained with his Battalion throughout. On January 7th 1916, he was struck in the head by an enemy bullet and instantly killed while in the trenches west of Wytschaete, Belgium. He was buried in Plot X, Row C, Grave 7, La Laiterie Military Cemetery, West-Vlaanderen, Belgium.

Service number: 65825

Medals and Awards: 1914-1915 Star, British War Medal and Victory Medal (1914-1919).

RIDDELL, Gerald E. **Corporal**
7th Recon. **WWII**

Courtesy The Watchman

Gerald Everrett Riddell was born in Crossfield, Alberta on March 23rd 1922, son of Horace and Olive Kerr. Gerald resided in Alberta for only two years then moved with his family to Lachute. His father was from Milles Isles and his mother from Lakefield and had been married in Montreal in 1922. Gerald attended Public School for seven years then High School for another four leaving school at age 18. He was then employed by K.A. McOuat of Lachute as a dairy driver. On September 9th 1942, he enlisted with the Canadian Armoured Corps in Montreal. At the time of his enlistment he was residing with his parents at 323 Main Street in Lachute. His brother, Clayton, also enlisted in the Royal Canadian Air Force and served overseas. He survived the War. Gerald was immediately assigned to No.4 District Depot in Montreal waiting for his training to begin. On September 19th, he was sent to No.48 Training Centre in St-Jean, Quebec. On November 18th, Trooper Riddell was sent to No.A-27 Training Centre in Dundurn, Saskatchewan for his Canadian Armoured Corps training. On March 19th 1943, he was promoted to Lance Corporal. Eight days later he boarded a troopship and made the crossing of the Atlantic without incidents, arriving safely in the United Kingdom on April 4th. Sadly, on October 21st 1943, his father, Horace, died. On arrival he was assigned to No.1 Canadian Armoured Corps Reinforcement Unit. He remained with this unit until June 4th, when he was transferred to the 7th Reconnaissance Regiment. He remained in the United Kingdom, training and getting ready for the attack on mainland Europe which was to come in the near future. On July 11th 1944, Trooper Riddell and the 7th Reconnaissance Regiment landed in France to fight the German Armies. On July 26th, he was promoted to Acting Corporal. On August 24th 1944, A/Corp. Gerald Everrett Riddell was killed in action in the vicinity of Orbec, France. He was initially buried in La Joquetterie, France but was later exhumed and reburied in Plot XXIV, Row E, Grave 3, Bretteville-Sur-Laize Canadian War Cemetery, Calvados, France.

Service number: D131299

Medals and Awards: 1939-45 Star, France and Germany Star, Defence Medal, the Canadian Volunteer Service Medal and clasp and the War Medal 1939-45.

ROBERTS, Alvin C. **Private**
R.H.R. **WWII**

Alvin Charles Roberts was born in Brownsburg on April 15th 1907, son of Charles, a paving cutter and Mary MacDonald, widow of George Fisher. Alvin was the half-brother of Norman Fisher who was killed in action in France in 1916. Another brother, Robert E., would enlist into the United States Army and served Overseas. Alvin remained in Argenteuil County and attended public school but left at the age of 13. Between 1920 and 1939 he was employed as a paving stone cutter with several quarry companies. From 1939 to his enlistment, he was employed by Canadian Industries Limited (C.I.L.), in Brownsburg, as a storekeeper of raw materials. On August 12th 1941, he enlisted with the Canadian Army in Montreal and was taken on strength with No.4 District Depot. On the 29th, he was sent to No.41 Basic Training Centre in Huntingdon, Quebec until October 30th, when he was sent for further training to No.A12 Advance Training Centre in Farnham, Quebec. He remained in Canada until February 28th 1942, when he left Canada enroute for the United Kingdom, which he reached safely on March 9th. On arrival, he was sent to No.2 Canadian Infantry Reinforcement Unit in Witley, England for further training. On May 8th, he was transferred to his unit, the The Black Watch (Royal Highland Regiment) of Canada. He remained in England until July 6th 1944, when he crossed into France with his unit. On July 23rd, while the R.H.R. were at Hill 67 in France, at approximately 0400hrs, a German patrol of about 50 men infiltrated the Battalion's lines and attacked the Command Post. A strong, sharp battle occurred which lasted about 15 minutes. By the end, the Germans had lost 17 men killed, four wounded and 22 prisoners, while the R.H.R. suffered one dead soldier, Pte Roberts. He was temporarily buried in Plot I, Row 1, Grave 2, in a cemetery five yards north of the road from Ifs to Fleury-sur-Orne. He was later exhumed and re-burried in Plot I, Row H, Grave 9, Bretteville-Sur-Laize Canadian War Cemetery, Calvados, France.

Service number: D82971

Medals and Awards: 1939-45 Star, France and Germany Star, Defence Medal, the Canadian Volunteer Service Medal and clasp and the War Medal 1939-45.

Robillard, Timothé **L/Corporal**
22nd Bn **WWI**

Timothé Robillard was born on January 31st 1886, in Grenville, son of Timothé and Mary Malette. He enlisted with "B" Company of the 22nd Battalion, C.E.F on January 7th 1915, in Saint-Jean, Quebec. At the time of his enlistment, he reported being a joiner by trade and having had prior military service with the 65th Regiment in Montreal. He remained in Canada until May 20th 1915, when he boarded the troopship S.S. Saxonia, arriving safely in England on the 29th. He remained with his Battalion in England until September 15th, when he crossed into France, landing in Boulogne. He was promoted to L/Cpl on December 2nd. On December 30th 1915, L/Cpl Robillard was killed in action, while in the trenches in the vicinity of Locre, Belgium. He was buried in Plot VII, Row A, Grave 2, La Laiterie Military Cemetery, West-Vlaanderen, Belgium.

Service number: 61619

Medals and Awards: 1914-1915 Star, British War Medal and Victory Medal (1914-1919).

ROBINSON, Donald W.B. R.C.A.F. | **F/Officer WWII**

LAC/BAC

Donald William Burroughs Robinson was born in Toronto, Ontario on April 30th 1925, son of Joseph Nicol, a draughtsman, and Maggie May Howell. He attended Primary School in Sioux Lookout, Ontario from 1931 to 1939 and High School in Fort William, also in Ontario, from 1940 to 1942. He joined No.66 Air Cadet Squadron in September 1942 still in Fort William. Donald enlisted with the Royal Canadian Air Force in Montreal on February 3rd, 1943. By that time, his mother had passed away in 1936 and his father was residing in Brownsburg. Upon enlistment, he was immediately assigned to No.5 Manning Depot in Lachine, Quebec until April 8th, when he was assigned to No.4 Bombing and Gunnery School in Fingal, Ontario. His training continued and after attending a few other training units, on June 23rd, he was sent to No.1 Initial Training School in Toronto. Throughout the rest of 1943 and until spring of 1944 his training continued, being assigned to several schools. On April 29th 1944, he embarked on a troopship in Halifax, Nova Scotia bound for the United Kingdom. He reached the safety of England on May 7th and was assigned the next day to No.3 Personnel Reception Centre in Bournemouth. Further training awaited him and he was posted to several training squadrons until February 25th, 1945 when he was transferred to No.424 Squadron, R.C.A.F. at Skipton-On-Swale, England. On March 7th 1945, 424 Squadron was detailed to take part in a 526 bomber raid on the city of Dessau, Germany. F/O Robinson was the navigator on board a Lancaster I bomber, serial NG-457. While enroute to the target, his aircraft was hit by enemy anti-aircraft fire and crashed near Dabringhausen, Germany. All but one, were killed. F/O Donald William Burroughs Robinson was only 19 years old. He, as well as four of his crew, were buried by the Germans in a communal grave in the Dabringhausen-Grunewald Roman Catholic cemetery. After the War, his body was respectfully exhumed and reburied in Plot XI, Row A, Grave 11, Rheinberg War Cemetery, Nordrhein-Westfalen, Germany.

Service number: J40915

Medals and Awards: 1939-45 Star, France and Germany Star, Defence Medal, the Canadian

Volunteer Service Medal and clasp and the War Medal 1939-45.

RUDDIMAN, William **Private**
2nd C.R.T. **WWI**

William Ruddiman was born on June 23rd 1874, in Aberdeen, Scotland, the son of John and Elizabeth Topp. William grew up in Scotland and became a stone mason like his father. He married Williamina Copeland on December 13th 1895, in Aberdeen. William immigrated to Canada in 1907, when he boarded the S.S. Numidian and arrived in Montreal on May 21st. On June 7th 1910, William's wife and children joined him in Canada and the family moved to Brownsburg. Sadly, one year later, William's wife died. William remarried some time after his first wife's death. By 1913, William was residing on St-Antoine Street in Montreal. His son, John, enlisted with the 148th Overseas Battalion on March 6th 1916, in Lachute. He survived the War. William enlisted with the 1st Construction Battalion, C.E.F., on August 3rd 1916. He remained in Canada until September 13th, when he boarded the troopship S.S. Northland, and arrived safely in England, disembarking in Liverpool on the 23rd. On October 21st, he was transferred to the 127th Battalion in Witley, England. William remained in England until January 12th 1917, when he proceeded to France, landing in Le Havre with the 127th. The very next day, the 127th was renamed the 2nd Battalion, Canadian Railway Troops. On February 4th, while in the vicinity of Acheux, France, William was injured by falling chalk while engaged in an excavating operation. He died the next day while at No.54 Field Ambulance. He was buried in Row L, Grave 13, Aveluy Communal Cemetery Extension, Somme, France.

Service number: 1081971

Medals and Awards: British War Medal and Victory Medal (1914-1919).

RUSSELL, Walter **Private**
60th Bn **WWI**

Walter Russell was born on November 3rd 1882, in Lee, Kent, England. He immigrated to Canada in 1905 and by 1911 was residing in Brownsburg with George and Belinda Rushbrook. At that time he was employed at the Cartridge Factory as an operative. Walter enlisted with "B" Company, 60th Battalion, C.E.F., on November 5th 1915, in Montreal. On his attestation papers, he is listed as having served for three years with the Royal Field Artillery. The very next day he boarded the troopship S.S. Scandinavian bound for England, arriving safely on the 15th. He remained in England with his Battalion until they crossed into France, landing in Le Havre on February 20th 1916. On May 5th 1916, Pte Walter Russell was killed in action South of Vlamertinghe, Belgium, when the camp he was in was hit by enemy artillery. He was buried in Plot I, Row D, Grave 34, Poperinghe New Military Cemetery, West-Vlaanderen, Belgium.

Service number: 458649

Medals and Awards: British War Medal and Victory Medal (1914-1919).

RYAN, Francis B. **Private**
13th Bn **WWI**

Francis Berton Ryan was born on September 26th 1882, in Upper Prospect, Halifax County, Nova

Scotia. On April 13th 1916, he enlisted with the 148th Overseas Battalion, C.E.F., in Lachute. By then he was residing in Brownsburg, was a barber by trade and had seen prior military service in Halifax. He remained in Canada until September 2nd 1917, when he boarded the troopship H.M.T. Megantic, en route for the War. His troopship arrived safely in Liverpool, England on the 15th. Once in England, he was assigned to the Canadian Forestry Corps in Sunningdale. On November 8th, he was posted to No. 128 Company, C.F.C. in Nairn, Scotland. His Company moved to Stirling, Scotland on the 19th. He remained assigned to the C.F.C. until he was transferred to the 20th Reserve Battalion in Bramshott, England on June 4th 1918. He arrived in France on September 12th, and joined the 13th Battalion on the 21st. On October 12th 1918, Pte Ryan was wounded by gas shells while his Battalion was in the vicinity of Sailly, France. He was evacuated to No. 13 General Hospital where he died four days later. He was buried in Plot V, Row F, Grave 6, Terlincthun British Cemetery, Wimille, Pas-de-Calais, France.

Service number: 842054

Medals and Awards: British War Medal and Victory Medal (1914-1919).

SCOTT, Wilbert J. **Private**
C.A.S.C. **WWI**

Wilbert Joseph Scott was born in Arundel on January 10th 1898, son of Albert Emmanuel and Mary Ann Bagley. By 1916, Wilbert was residing in Montreal with his father. On January 17th 1916, he enlisted with No.3 Company, 3rd Divisional Train, Canadian Expeditionary Force, in Montreal. At that time, he reported being a shipper and having served nine months with No.15 Canadian Army Service Corps. He remained in Canada until he boarded the troopship S.S. Scandinavian and arrived safely in England on March 12th. On April 3rd, he made the crossing and arrived in Le Havre, France, joining the 3rd Divisional Train and was attached to the 9th Field Ambulance. On October 1st 1918, he was severely wounded by gunshot to his hip and abdomen. He was evacuated to the War Hospital in Bradford, England for treatment. Sadly, on the 18th, Pte Wilbert Joseph Scott succumbed to his wounds. He was buried in Plot K, Row U, Grave 609, Bradford (Scholemoor) Cemetery, Yorkshire, United Kingdom.

Service number: 511721

Medals and Awards: British War Medal and Victory Medal (1914-1919).

SEWELL, Vernon **Sergeant**
R.C.A.F. **WWII**

Vernon Young Hodgson Sewell was born in Newark, Ohio, United States, on October 2nd 1914, son of Mayson Hodgson, a Presbyterian Minister and Emma Lydia Young. Vernon's parents were both born in England. He attended Elmira High School, in Elmira Ontario, from 1929 to 1933, then Cumberland University in Tennessee, from 1933 to 1934, and obtained his Bachelor of Law Degree. Vernon then attended several lectures in aeronautics at McGill University, in Montreal, from 1936 to 1937. Vernon joined the Montreal Light Aeroplane Club in 1936, and flew fifteen hours in dual and five hours in solo training. He was training with the Moth and Fleet Trainer aircrafts. From 1937 up until his enlistment, he was employed by

Canadian Industries Limited (C.I.L.) in Brownsburg as a private secretary. Vernon was naturalized a British subject in 1937. On May 29th 1940, he enlisted with the Royal Canadian Air Force in Montreal. At the time of his enlistment, he reported residing in Brownsburg and, his parents, in Montreal. He was immediately assigned to No.1 Manning Depot in Toronto. Two days later he was sent to No.1 Initial Training School. His training continued. On June 21st, he was sent to No.1 Wireless School in Montreal. On November 9th, he was sent to No.1 Bombing and Gunnery School in Jarvis, Ontario. On December 15th, he was promoted to Sergeant and awarded an air gunner's badge. On the 27th, he was sent to R.C.A.F. Station Rockcliffe, Ottawa, Ontario. He remained in Canada until February 7th 1941, when he sailed across the Atlantic and disembarked safely in the United Kingdom on the 15th where he was assigned to No.19 Operational Training Unit. On July 22nd, Sgt Sewell was transferred to No.10 R.A.F. Squadron at R.A.F. Leeming. On the night of August 16th 1941, Sgt Sewell was a member of a crew of a Whitley V bomber number Z6794. The aircraft took off from Leeming at 2209hrs, for a bombing attack on the city of Cologne, Germany. Over the target area, it was reported that the flak defense was intense and accurate. Sgt Sewell's aircraft crashed near Nieukerk, Germany. He and another were killed while four others of the crew were taken prisoners. He was buried in Grave 8 in the Military Cemetery in Nieukerk, District of Geldern, Germany. He was later exhumed after the War and re-interred in Plot 25, Row F, Grave 18, Reichswald Forest War Cemetery, Nordrhein-Westfalen, Germany.

Service Number: R54577

Medals and Awards: 1939-45 Star, Air Crew Europe Star, the Canadian Volunteer Service Medal and clasp and the War Medal 1939-45.

SILVERSON, Wilbert W. C.E. **Driver WWI**

Wilbert Wesley Silverson was born in Huberdeau on August 10th 1897, son of John and Elizabeth Staniforth. He remained with his family until 1911. By 1916, he found himself in Alberta, enlisting with the 66th Battalion, C.E.F. on March 6th, in Edmonton. At the time of his enlistment, he was residing in Bashaw, Alberta and worked as a farmer. He remained in Canada for the next couple of months, until May 1st, when he boarded the troopship S.S. Olympic, arriving safely in England on the 7th. On the 21st, he was transferred to the Canadian Engineers Training Depot in Shorncliffe. On October 14th, he was transferred to the 7th Field Company and arrived in France two days later. He remained with this Engineers unit until he was transferred to the 3rd Pontoon Bridging and Transport Unit, Canadian Engineers, on May 30th 1918. He remained with this unit for the duration of the War. He survived past November 11th, but sadly, on February 24th 1919, on returning from leave, he was admitted to the 2nd Scottish General Hospital in Edinburgh, where he died of ptomaine (food) poisoning. On July 3rd 1919, he was awarded the Military Medal posthumously. He was buried in Plot D Grave 32, Comely Bank Cemetery, Edinburgh, Scotland.

Service number: 101717

Medals and Awards: Military Medal, British War Medal and Victory Medal (1914-1919).

SMITH, James E. **Private**
1st Q.R. **WWI**

James Earnest Smith was born on April 9th 1896, in Cushing, son of Walter and Mary Elizabeth Knox. He remained with his parents until he was drafted into the 1st Depot Battalion, 1st Quebec Regiment on July 13th 1918. James never made it to Europe and the War. He was still in Canada by War's end and sadly, on January 21st 1919, he died of influenza. He was buried in the Protestant cemetery in St-Andrews East.

Service number: 3087178

Medals and Awards: Nil

STANIFORTH, Charles H. **Private**
24th Bn **WWI**

Charles Harry Staniforth was born in Arundel on April 7th 1893, son of Frank and Catherine Strong. He remained with his parents, until he enlisted with the 148th Overseas Battalion, on March 15th 1916, in Montreal. Charles had served a few days in the 17th Hussars prior to his enlistment. He remained in Canada until September 27th, when he boarded the troopship S.S. Laconia in Halifax, and landed safely in Liverpool, England on October 6th. He remained in England, and was transferred to the 24th Battalion on December 5th, while in Witley Camp. Two days later, he joined his new Battalion in the battlefields of France. On August 15th 1917, the 24th Battalion was part of the Canadian Expeditionary Force's attack on Hill 70. Pte Charles Staniforth was killed in action during this attack. Charles has no known grave and is commemorated on the Vimy Memorial, Pas-de-Calais, France.

Service number: 841801

Medals and Awards: British War Medal and Victory Medal (1914-1919).

STAPLETON, Robert B. **Private**
C.R.T. **WWI**

Robert Boyd Stapleton was born in Arundel on November 4th 1897, son of Henry and Nellie Boyd. Robert enlisted with No. 58 Broad Gauge Railway Operating Company, Canadian Railway Troops, C.E.F. on January 26th 1917, in Montreal. On enlistment, he declared residing at 158 Mount Royal Avenue in Montreal with his mother and being a fireman by trade. He remained in Canada for a couple of months until March 4th, when he boarded the troopship S.S. Aussonia in Halifax. The crossing of the Atlantic was made safely and Robert landed in England on the 15th. His stay in England was short lived: on April 17th, he boarded a ship and he crossed the Channel and landed in France two days later. On October 26th 1918, Pte Stapleton was sent to No. 37 Casualty Clearing Station suffering from ascitis. On November 2nd, he was admitted to No. 11 Stationary Hospital in Rouen, France. His condition deteriorated rapidly and was listed as being dangerously ill on December 14th. Sadly, two days later, Pte Stapleton died at the hospital. He was buried in Plot S, Row III, Grave CC 5, St Sever cemetery Extension, Rouen, Seine-Maritime, France.

Service number: 2124932

Medals and Awards: British War Medal and Victory Medal (1914-1919).

STILWELL, Frank S. **R.C.D.**

Lieutenant **Korea**

LAC/BAC

Frank Sidney Stilwell was born in Brownsburg on November 20th 1924, son of Sidney Henri and Irene Neveu. He grew up in Brownsburg, attending School from 1931 to 1941 and high School in Lachute from 1941 to 1942. On leaving school, he was employed as a tool maker with C.I.L. in Brownsburg. On November 20th 1942, Frank enlisted in the Royal Canadian Air Force in Montreal, and remained attached with No.13 Recruiting Centre until he was sent to No.5 Manning Depot in Lachine, on February 22nd 1943. From Lachine, he was sent to No.4 Wireless School in Guelph, Ontario, on April 15th; to No.6 Initial Training School in Toronto, on June 26th; arriving at No.10 Elemental Flying Training School in Pendleton, Ontario on September 5th. His training was far from completed. On November 14th, he was then sent to No.1 Service Flying Training School at Camp Borden, Ontario. On April 7th 1944, Frank was commissioned a Pilot Officer after having graduated as a fighter pilot the day before, qualified on Harvard and Hurricane aircrafts. He remained in Canada, being assigned to several units until March 18th 1945, when he boarded a troopship bound for the United Kingdom. He arrived safely on the 26th, and assigned to No.3 Personnel Reception Centre in Bournemouth, England. He never made it to an operational squadron by War's end and was returned to Canada after the end of hostilities, where he was transferred to the general section of reserve Class "E" on September 7th, 1945.

In 1946, he returned to school, this time attending Sir George William's College in Montreal, studying maths and physics until 1948. On December 28th 1946, Frank married Marie Tetu in Montreal.

In June 1950, the Korean Peninsula found itself at war. In 1951, Frank, once again, enlisted with the Canadian military, this time with the Royal Canadian Armored Corps on January 8th, as a 2nd/Lieutenant, in Montreal. He was transferred to the Royal Canadian Dragoons in Petawawa, Ontario on June 10th. He remained in Petawawa until January 14th 1952, when he was sent for training at the Canadian Joint Air Training Centre in Rivers, Manitoba, returning to his unit in Petawawa on July 31st. He remained in Canada until June 18th 1953, when he left Canada for Japan, arriving safely on the 20th. He remained in Japan until he was sent to Korea on November 29th, and was assigned to Headquarters, 25 Canadian Infantry Brigade. On January 25th 1954, at 0800hrs, Lieutenant Frank Sidney Stilwell was found dead in his bed. The primary cause of death was found to have been coronary insufficiency. He was buried on January 30th, in Plot 38, Row 4, Grave 3212, Canvas Square, in the United Nations Military Cemetery in Tang-gok, Korea.

Service number: J44057/ZD3896

Medals and awards: The Canadian Volunteer Service Medal and clasp, the War Medal 1939-45 and the United Nations Service Medal.

STRONG, Randolph W. **Lieutenant**
C.F.C. **WWI**

McGill Honour Roll
1914-1918

Randolph William Strong was born in Cambria, Mille-Isles on July 28th 1890, son of Matthew, a mill owner and Martha Beckham. In 1909, he was admitted in the Faculty of Applied Sciences at McGill University in Montreal. While in Montreal he joined the Montreal Heavy Brigade, a militia artillery unit. On April 28th 1916, Randolph enlisted in the No.6 McGill Overseas Battery, Siege Artillery, C.E.F. He followed in the footsteps of his older brother, Garnet Matthew, who had enlisted with the 5th Pioneer Battalion a month prior. (Garnet would survive the War, promoted to the rank of Lieut. Colonel, was Mentioned in Despatches by General Haig (1917) and awarded a Distinguished Service Order (1918)). He remained in Canada until September 18th, when he boarded the troopship S.S. Olympic in Halifax and landed safely in England on the 25th. On arrival he was transferred to the 271st Siege Battery. On January 24th 1917, the 271st was renamed the 7th Canadian Siege Battery. On March 14th, Randolph and his unit proceeded to France and the War. On April 28th, he suffered a shrapnel wound to his left arm and was evacuated to the 2nd Western General Hospital in Manchester, England. He remained in England for treatment and recuperation and was transferred to the Canadian Forestry Corps on October 13th. Two weeks later, on the 27th, he was commissioned and appointed as a temporary lieutenant. Following his promotion, he was assigned to No. 134, No. 123 Companies and No. 54 District, C.F.C. in

Southampton, England. On July 16th 1918, he was admitted to Granville Canadian Special Hospital in Buxton, having suffered a stroke. On July 26th, at 0645hrs, Lieutenant Randolph William Strong died of embolic hemiplegia. He was buried in Grave 2478, Buxton cemetery, Derbyshire, United Kingdom.

Service number: 1261671

Medals and Awards: British War Medal and Victory Medal (1914-1919).

TASSE, Roger | **Private**
Régt. Châteauguay | **WWII**

William Jean Roger Tassé was born in Brownsburg on October 7th 1921, son of Théodore and Corine Lacasse. He completed seven years of public school in Brownsburg, leaving at the age of 15. In 1937, he began employment with Canadian Industries Limited in Brownsburg, as a tool setter. On September 14th 1942, he was drafted under the authority of the National Resources Mobilization Act. On the 26th, he was sent to No.45 Training Centre in Sorel, Quebec. On January 31st 1943, he was transferred to the Régiment de Châteauguay in St-John, New-Brunswick until July 15th, when he was sent to Goose Bay in Labrador and joined No.5 Aerodrome Defence Company. Pte Tassé started to be ill and after a medical examination, was found to no longer be fit for further military service. He was discharged from the Army on July 11th 1944, in Montreal. Private Tassé died on January 23rd 1945, in Ste-Anne-de-Bellevue, Quebec. The causes of death were cited as being generalized peritonitis and abscess of the left kidney, and were due to military service. He was buried in the St-Louis de France cemetery in Brownsburg.

Service number: D638408

Medals and Awards: War Medal 1939-1945

TESSIER, Lorenzo **Private**
R22eR **WWII**

Courtesy Lynn Vallée

Lorenzo Tessier was born on June 26th 1913, in St-André-Avellin, son of Jean-Baptiste, a farmer and Emélia Hotte. Prior to his enlistment, he worked as an electrician in Montreal. He enlisted in the Canadian Army on July 1st 1940, and was assigned to the Royal 22e Régiment. He married Marguerite Jolin, from Lachute, on the 30th of December 1940, in L'Abord-à-Plouffe, Laval, Quebec. He spent his first years in Canada, attending numerous courses and was promoted to Corporal on April 1st 1943. Another promotion followed suit since, on May 20th, he was promoted to the rank of Acting/Sergeant. Lorenzo Tessier was sent overseas and landed in Great-Britain on December 21st, where he was attached to No.5 Canadian Infantry Reinforcement Unit at Tourney Barracks, Aldershot, England. On his arrival to Great-Britain, he reverted to his confirmed rank of Corporal. He remained with No.5 C.I.R.U. until January 14th 1944, when he was assigned to Headquarters, First Canadian Army. Three days later, he reverted to the rank of Private at his own request. Pte Tessier was sent to the Mediterranean Theater of Operations where, on

March 22nd, he rejoined his original unit, the Royal 22e Régiment in Italy. On April 19th, he wrote his last letter to his wife from a trench hole. Lorenzo told his wife that the artillery was raining down on them and he was hunkering down. His letter is a testament to the hardships and dangers men like Lorenzo endured. On May 19th 1944, Pte Lorenzo Tessier was killed in action, during the Regiment`s attack on the Hitler Line. He was buried in Plot IX, Row K, Grave 17, Cassino War Cemetery, Italy.

Service number: D106181

Medals and awards: 1939-45 Star, Italy Star, the Canadian Volunteer Service Medal and clasp and the War Medal 1939-45.

THEORET, Joseph C. **L.A.C.**
R.C.A.F. **WWII**

LAC/BAC

Joseph Charles Hormidas Théoret was born in Toronto, Ontario on October 30th 1921, son of Joseph Hormidas, a veterinarian and Blanche Guillet. By 1928, this family had moved to Quebec. Joseph Charles attended St-Dominic Academy primary school in Montreal from 1928 to 1935 and the High School in Lachute, graduating in 1940. Also in 1940, he became employed by the Bank of Nova Scotia, Lachute branch, as a collection clerk. Joseph Charles enlisted in the Royal Canadian Air Force on June 27th 1941, in Montreal. He was assigned to No.4 Auxiliary Manning Depot in St-Hubert, Quebec, upon enlistment. He remained in St-Hubert until

August 8th, when he was sent to No.8 Service Flying Training School in Moncton, New-Brunswick. His pilot training was beginning. On October 10th, he was sent to No.3 Initial Training School in Victoriaville, Quebec where his flight training continued. He remained in Victoriaville until December 21st, when he was posted to No.4 Elemental Flying Training School in Windsor Mills, Quebec. On March 15th 1942, he was sent to No.13 Service Flying Training School in St-Hubert. On June 16th 1942, LAC Joseph Charles Théoret was killed during a night dual instructional flight. The Harvard aircraft he was receiving instructions in ran out of fuel and crashed in the area of Ragged Lake Mountain, near Malone, New-York, USA. He was buried in the Ste-Anastasie cemetery in Lachute.

Service number: R108354

Medals and Awards: The Canadian Volunteer Service Medal and War Medal 1939-45.

TOWNSEND, Warren E. **Sapper**
R.C.E. **WWII**

Warren Ernest Townsend was born in Ogdensburg on May 14th 1921, son of Ernest Samuel, a farm labourer and Sylvia Inman. Warren attended Public School until the age of 16. He later went to work as a labourer in a sawmill with McGibbon's in Lachute and Cyril Gagne from St-Michel, Quebec. On July 6th 1942, Warren enlisted under the authority of the National Resources Mobilization Act of 1940, and was immediately taken on strength with No.4 District Depot in Montreal. A week later, on the 14th, he was sent to Petawawa, Ontario and posted to the 74th Battery, 6th Anti-tank Regiment. On the 27th, Gunner Townsend attested into the Canadian Army Active Service and remained with the 74th Battery. His brother Harold also saw service during WWII and survived the War. On November 28th 1942, Warren married Miss Clara Marion who was residing in Pembroke. He remained in Canada until August 24th 1943, when he boarded a ship and left Canada, arriving safely in the United Kingdom on September 1st. On January 3rd 1944, he was transferred to the Canadian Army Service Corps Reinforcement Unit in Farnborough, England. On April 14th, he was again transferred, this time to the 4th Light Anti-Aircraft Regiment. Warren and the 4th landed in Normandy on June 10th, four days after the storming of the beaches by the Allies. On September 24th, he was transferred to the 16th Field Company, Royal Canadian Engineers, as a cook. On October 6th 1944, "Operation Switchback", the assault of the Scheldt Estuary began, and it was during that battle that Pte Warren Townsend was wounded in the vicinity of the Leopold Canal, Belgium. He died the same day. He was buried in Plot VIII, Row F, Grave 8, Adegem Canadian War Cemetery, Oost-Vlaanderen, Belgium.

Service number: D156022

Medals and Awards: 1939-45 Star, France and Germany Star, Defence Medal, the Canadian Volunteer Service Medal and clasp and the War Medal 1939-45

WARD, Russell M. **R.H.R.** | **Private** **WWII**

Courtesy RCL Lachute

Russell Melvin Ward was born in Côte St-Luc, Quebec on August 16th 1916, son of Ernest James and Laura Matilda Lyster. The family moved to Lachute where Russell completed his public school at age 13. On November 25th 1939, Russell married Eunice Alma MacRae in Lachute. At that time he was employed as a transport chauffeur. In 1942, he started employment as a store clerk in an ammunition plant with Canadian Industries Limited out of Brownsburg. On June 8th 1943, Russell enlisted, in Hawkesbury Ontario, with the 2nd Battalion, Stormont, Dundas and Glengarry Highlanders, a Reserve Regiment of the Non-Permanent Active Militia of Canada. He completed several months of training with this Regiment, until October 25th, when he enlisted with the Canadian Army in Montreal South and assigned to No.4 District Depot. At the time of his enlistment, he reported residing at 113 Robert Street in Lachute. Two of his younger brothers, Lyster Ernest and Howard William also enlisted in the Canadian Army. Both survived the War. On November 5th, Russell was sent to No.A-19 Canadian Army Service Corps Training Centre in Camp Borden, Ontario. This lasted until the end of December when, on the 30th, he was sent to No.48 Training Centre in St-Jean, Quebec, for the beginning of infantry training. On February 13th 1944, he was sent to Farnham, Quebec to continue that training. Pte Ward left Canada on April 30th 1944, and sailed for the United Kingdom. He landed safely on May 7th, where he joined No.4 Canadian Infantry

Reinforcement Unit. On June 22nd, he was transferred to the 1st Battalion, The Black Watch (Royal Highland Regiment) of Canada, and arrived in France on July 6th. On July 25th 1944, The Black Watch (Royal Highland Regiment) of Canada took part in a disastrous attack at May-Sur-Orne, France. It was during this attack that Pte Russell Melvin Ward was killed in action. He was temporarily buried in Plot 2, Row 3, Grave 20, Saint-Martin-de-Fontenay cemetery on August 14th. He was later exhumed and re-burried in Plot I, Row E, Grave 7, Bretteville-Sur-Laize Canadian War Cemetery, Calvados, France.

Service number: D143305

Medals and Awards: 1939-45 Star, France and Germany Star, the Canadian Volunteer Service Medal and clasp and the War Medal 1939-45.

WATSON, Robert M. **Sergeant**
R.C.A.F. **WWII**

LAC/BAC

Robert Martin Watson was born in St-Andrews East on February 9th 1921, son of William George, a farmer and Cecilia Mary Albright. By 1944, Robert's parents were residing in Lachute. He attended the St-Andrews East Consolidated School from 1928 to 1937, and then was employed on his father's farm until 1939. After farm work he began employment with Canadian Vickers, out of Montreal, as a shipwright helper, position he held until his enlistment. On April 20th 1942, he enlisted with the Royal Canadian Air Force in Montreal, and was taken on strength with No.5 Manning Depot in Lachine, Quebec. On July 4th, he was sent to No.4 Wireless School in Guelph, Ontario until February 7th 1943, when he was sent to No.9 Bombing and Gunnery School in Mont-Joli, Quebec. He travelled to the United States and, on May 4th, he left New-York, and crossed the Atlantic, landing safely in the United Kingdom on the 11th, being assigned to No.3 Personnel Reception Centre in Bournemouth, England. From No.3 P.R.C., he was transferred to No.19 Operational Training Unit, No.1663 Conversion Unit, and finally to No.76 Squadron, Royal Air Force, on September 21st, at Holme-on-Spalding Moor, England. On October 3rd 1943, 76 Squadron was part of a 547 bomber raid on Kassel, Germany. Sgt Robert Martin Watson was a crew member on board a Halifax bomber, number DK247, which took off from Holme-on-Spalding Moor at 1830hrs. This aircraft was shot down by a JU88C-6 D5 LK flown by Fw Frank, and crashed in the vicinity of Vehne Moor, south-west of Oldenburg, Germany. Sgt Watson was instantly killed. He was buried in Row 10, Grave 29, Allied Plot, New Cemetery in Oldenburg, Germany. He was later exhumed and reburied in Plot 1, Row D, Grave 8, Sage War Cemetery, Niedersachsen, Germany.

Service number: R164504

Medals and Awards: 1939-45 Star, Air Crew Europe Star, the Canadian Volunteer Service Medal and clasp and the War Medal 1939-45.

WERT, Gerald H. **Private**
C & Y Regt. **WWII**

Gerald Hugh Wert was born in Lachute on February 14th 1916, son of Walter, a lumberman, and Jessie Lucretia Morrow. He attended school until grade nine. From 1929 to 1939 he was employed as a lumberjack for several companies. Gerald enlisted with the Canadian Army on September 27th 1939, in Montreal. His brother Carl also enlisted with the Canadian Army and survived the War. Gerald was immediately assigned to the 1st Battalion, The Black Watch (Royal Highland Regiment) of Canada in Montreal. On March 29th 1940, he was then in Toronto, Ontario with his unit. By June 8th, Pte Wert found himself in Valcartier, Quebec. From Valcartier, he was sent to Newfoundland, Halifax and Aldershot, Nova-Scotia. On August 22nd, he boarded a troopship and left Canada arriving safely in Gourock Scotland on September 4th. Pte Wert remained in the United Kingdom training for the War. On April 25th 1942, he married Violet Edith Lively of England. On March 2nd, he was transferred to No.5 Canadian Infantry Reinforcement Unit at Tourney Barracks, Aldershot, England. He remained with this unit until June 4th, when he was transferred to the Carleton and York Regiment. Pte Wert left the United Kingdom on June 30th, and landed in Sicily on July 11th, during the Allied amphibious assault codenamed "Husky". On December 13th 1943, Pte Gerald Hugh Wert was wounded in action while the Carleton and York were engaged in battle against German forces in the vicinity of San Leonardo and Ortona crossroads. The battalion ran into heavy opposition and were hit by enemy mortars, machineguns, artillery and tanks. They failed to capture their objectives and suffered casualties. Pte Gerald Hugh Wert died as a result of his wounds and was buried the same day in the South Apollinan cemetery in Italy until he was later exhumed and reburied in Plot XI, Row A, Grave 11, Moro River Canadian War Cemetery, Italy.

Service number: D81731

Medals and Awards: 1939-45 Star, Italy Star, Defence Medal, the Canadian Volunteer Service Medal and clasp and the War Medal 1939-45.

WHITE, John B. C.F.C. **Maj/General WWII**

Courtesy White Family

John Burton White was born on Aylmer Road, Wright, Quebec on January 1st 1874, son of Henry and Amelia Kelly. He went to public and high schools, then attended the Ottawa Business College leaving at age 20. He began his career in the lumber trade in 1896, when he entered business with the Hull Lumber Company, as a clerk in the lumber camps and worked his way to manager. On April 18th 1906, John married Margaret Jane Ferguson in Mattawa, Ontario. John would remain in the lumber business, working for several lumber companies, to eventually rise to the vice-presidency of the Canadian International Paper Company. By 1911, John Burton and his family were residing at Lot 18 Concession 2, Grenville Township and he was a manager of a lumber company. John's military career began in 1912, when he joined the 17th Duke of York Royal Canadian Hussars, a Canadian militia unit. He was commissioned as a Lieutenant on May 1st. His military career would take off henceforth. He was promoted to Captain on May 2nd 1914, and then to Major on August 27th 1915, commanding "B" Squadron. On March 1st 1916, he enlisted with the 224th Forestry Battalion, Canadian Expeditionary Force with the rank of Major, in

Ottawa. At the time of his enlistment, he reported residing in Westmount, Quebec with his wife. On April 18th, he left Canada and crossed the Atlantic arriving safely in the United Kingdom on the 28th. On May 1st, he was transferred to Headquarters in London from Larkhill Camp, England. Major White crossed into France and landed on June 7th. He remained in France with the 224th Battalion only a short period, since, on July 5th, he was sent to Canada, arriving safely on the 16th. He had been promoted to Lieutenant Colonel on June 1st and had been assigned to raise and command the 242nd Forestry Battalion. The Battalion was raised in the Montreal area, and Lt-Col White found himself returning to England and France. In January 1917, he was appointed as Director of Timber Operations in England, and in June of the same year, Director of Timber Operations in France. His work was obviously seen as exemplary. On November 7th 1917, he was Mentioned in Despatches, awarded the Distinguished Service Order on January 1st 1918, and again Mentioned in Despatches for valuable services rendered, on August 13th. On November 23rd, at War's end, Lt-Col White was promoted to Temporary Brigadier General. His War service hadn't gone unnoticed. In 1919 he was awarded the French Légion d'Honneur (Officier). He left Europe on September 4th 1919, boarding the R.M.S. Cedric in Liverpool, arriving safely in Halifax, Nova Scotia on the 12th. After his demobilization, John Burton reverted to the rank of Lt-Colonel and during the interwar years remained in the military, being appointed as Commanding Officer of the 3rd Mounted Brigade, and Honorary Lt-Colonel of the 17th Duke of York Royal Canadian Hussars of the Canadian Active Militia. In 1933, he was awarded the Efficiency Decoration and in 1935 the King's Silver Jubilee Medal.

On September 10th 1939, Canada found itself at war again against Germany. John was called to active service once again and on July 4th 1940, he enlisted with the Canadian Forestry Corps with the rank of Brigadier General, and was to be its Commanding Officer. Both his sons, Donald and Franklyn also enlisted in the Canadian Army and were commissioned as officers. Both survived the War. John Burton remained in Canada until December 15th, when he boarded a troopship in Halifax bound for the United Kingdom. He landed safely in Gourock, Scotland on the 24th, and assumed command of the Canadian Forestry Corps. On January 1st 1943, he was appointed a Commander of the Order of the British Empire (CBE). The award of the CBE was presented at the Investiture in England on February 2nd. The citation of this award speaks volume about this fine officer:

> *"Brigadier-General White who commanded the Canadian Forestry Corps in France in the last war was called upon to organize the Canadian Forestry Corps in this war. In the performance of this duty he has made an outstanding success. The Canadian Forestry Corps in the United Kingdom is a highly efficient organization which is making a most important contribution to the nation's war effort. For this efficiency General White is in a large measure personally responsible. He has carried out his duties with energy and decision. He has exhibited professional ability of the highest order."*

He remained in the United Kingdom until he was returned to Canada due to ill health in October of 1943. On the 14th, he was taken on strength with No.4 District Depot in Montreal. He was admitted to the Montreal General Hospital on October 16th, and was discharged on January 19th 1944. On June 19th, he retired from the Canadian Army. Major-General John Burton White died following illnesses in Montreal on May 31st 1945. The records indicate that death was due to his military service. He was buried on June 4th, in Lot 743, Section 12, Nepean (Merivale) cemetery, Ottawa, Ontario.

Service number: Major General

Medals and Awards: Commander of the Most Excellent Order of the British Empire (CBE), Companion of the Distinguished Service Order (DSO), twice Mentioned in Despatches, British War Medal, Allied Victory Medal (1914-1919), the Defence Medal, the Canadian Volunteer Service Medal and clasp, the War Medal (1939-45), 1935 Jubilee Medal, Efficiency Decoration, French Légion d'Honneur (Officier).

WHITESIDE, A. Barlow R.F.C. — Lieutenant WWI

Arthur Barlow Whiteside was born on December 13th 1891, in Fort Qu'Appelle, Saskatchewan, the son of Arthur, a Methodist Reverend and Henrietta Rebecca George. The Whitesides moved frequently, relocating in Saskatchewan, Alberta and in Inverness, Quebec. By 1911, Barlow was boarding at the residence of William Walker in Lachute. He was admitted to McGill University in the Faculty of Arts in 1912. When War broke out, he was quick to enlist. On September 23rd 1914, he enlisted with No.1 Canadian General Hospital, C.E.F. Pte Whiteside had served in the 11th Argenteuil Rangers from 1910 to 1912, so he was no stranger to the military life. He boarded the troopship S.S. Scandinavian in Quebec City on October 4th, and crossed the Atlantic bound for England and henceforth the War. The ship arrived safely in Plymouth on the 19th, and he entrained for Lavington. From Lavington, they marched to West Down North where they set up the hospital. Pte Whiteside remained in England until May 14th 1915, when his unit crossed the English Channel and landed in Boulogne, France. He remained with this unit until February 17th 1916, when he volunteered to be assigned to a combat unit: The P.P.C.L.I. On June 5th 1916, while in the Ypres Salient, Belgium, Pte Whiteside, was wounded by shrapnel to his left wrist and right arm. He was evacuated out of the frontlines and sent to Boulogne. From there he was sent back to England where he was taken to Lincoln on the 10th. His wounds were cared for and on July 12th, he was sent convalescing at the Canadian Convalescent Hospital, Woodcote Park, Epsom. He remained in other hospitals recuperating until he was assigned to the C.C.A.C. on January 2nd, 1917 in Hastings. He remained in England until March 17th, when he joined the Cadet Wing, Royal Flying Corps, in Denham Bucks. His flying career began. After completion, he went from Denham Bucks to the School of Military Aeronautics in Oxford. On May 9th, Pte Whiteside was discharged from the Canadian Expeditionary Force and was commissioned into the Royal Flying Corps as a Second Lieutenant the next day. On June 8th, 2/Lt Whiteside was assigned to No.9 Fighter Squadron at Estrées-en-Chaussée, France. Lt Whiteside continued flying with the Royal Flying Corps and after April 1st 1918, the Royal Air Force. After No.9 Squadron, he was assigned to No.51 and No.102 Squadrons respectively. He flew numerous and dangerous missions during the War and his bravery and dedication did not go unnoticed. On March 26th 1918, he was awarded the Military Cross. The citation accompanying the medal was gazetted in the London Gazette and read as follows:

> *"For conspicuous gallantry and devotion to duty. He carried out several night bombing raids with great success, attacking enemy aerodromes, trains and billets, often from a low altitude. On one occasion he attacked a train with his machine gun from a height of 100 feet. He showed splendid skill and initiative."*

Lt Whiteside continued flying missions with No.102 Squadron. He had a close call on May 23rd 1918, when, while accompanied by Lt E.F. Howard M.C., he was flying a FE2b aircraft on a night bombing mission, his propeller had been struck by shrapnel in the vicinity of Ficheux, France, which caused his engine to fail. He was able to land his crippled aircraft safely.

On September 16th 1918, he was again awarded a Military Cross and received a Bar. The London Gazette's citation speaks volume about the bravery and strength of character of Lt Whiteside:

> *"For conspicuous gallantry and devotion. This officer has taken part in over fifty night bombing raids many of which, carried out at heights considerable under 1,000 feet, and in adverse weather conditions, were only successful through the skill and energy displayed by him in discovering and attacking his objective. On one night in particular, after having successfully bombed a large ammunition dump, which was set on fire and blown up, he proceeded to drop bombs on a town which held large numbers of the enemy, also firing from a low altitude with*

his machine gun on the roads leading to it. Returning to his squadron, he obtained more bombs and ammunition, and with the same observer proceeded to drop bombs on a train behind enemy lines. On several occasions his machine was badly knocked about by enemy fire from the ground. The devotion to duty and disregard of danger displayed by this officer have been admirable examples to all members of his squadron."

On September 13th 1918, he was assigned to No.2 School of Navigation and Bomb Dropping as an instructor. He remained with this unit for the duration of the War and afterwards. On April 22nd 1919, he was one of several passengers in a Handley Page aircraft piloted by Major T.A. Batchelor, a Distinguished Flying Cross winner. The aircraft was taking off from Weyhill Aerodrome when it collided with buildings and crashed. Five were killed, including Lieut. Whiteside. The Court of Inquiry returned a verdict that the pilot had made an error in judgement. Lieut. Arthur Barlow Whiteside was buried in Penton Mewsey Holy Trinity Churchyard, Hampshire, United Kingdom.

Service number: 50009

Medals and Awards: Military Cross and Bar, 1914-15 Star, British War Medal and Victory Medal (1914-1919).

WHITTAL, Almer **Private**
1st Bn **WWI**

Almer Whittal was born on November 9th 1895, in Ormstown, Quebec. Very little is known of this soldier. He enlisted with the 87th Battalion,

Canadian Grenadier Guards, C.E.F. on November 11th 1915. At the time of his enlistment, he reported having been born in Ormstown, Quebec, but was residing in Lachute and worked as a farmer. He remained in Canada until he boarded the troopship S.S. Empress of Britain in Halifax on April 23rd 1916, and landed safely in Liverpool, England on May 5th. On June 19th, he joined the 1st Battalion in the field on the Western Front. On October 6th 1916, Pte Almer Whittal was killed in action while his Battalion was in the trenches in the vicinity of Albert, France. His body was never found and he is commemorated on the Vimy Memorial, Pas-de-Calais, France. His older brother, Bertie, enlisted with the C.E.F. on January 16th 1917 and survived the War.

Service number: 177504

Medals and Awards: British War Medal and Victory Medal (1914-1919).

WHYTOCK, Robert W. **F/Sergeant**
R.C.A.F. **WWII**

Courtesy of Editorial Board of West Hill

Robert William Roland Whytock was born in Montreal on November 23rd 1919, son of Robert Alexander, a car man with Canadian Pacific Railways and Laura Ann Matthew. Robert was baptized in Grenville, location of his mother's birth. He attended Gibson School from 1926 to 1933 and then West Hill High School in Montreal from 1933 to 1938. In 1938 he was employed by R.J Pickford in Montreal as an interior decorator. He remained with this company until August 1939, when Robert was employed by Canadian Lastex

Limited, also out of Montreal, in maintenance work. Robert enlisted with the Royal Canadian Air Force on August 20th 1940, in Montreal and was sent the next day to No.1 Manning Depot in Toronto. On the 31st, he was sent to Camp Borden, Ontario until October 13th, when he was sent to No.1 Initial Training School in Toronto. From there he was sent to No.1 Wireless School in Montreal until March 16th 1941, when he was sent to No.1 Bombing and Gunnery School in Jarvis, Ontario. On June 14th, he was transferred to the Royal Air Force Trainees Pool until July 17th, when he arrived in England and was sent to No.3 Personnel Reception Center in Bournemouth. On November 18th, he was transferred to No.14 Operational Training Unit until May 12th 1942, when he was assigned to No.420 R.C.A.F. Squadron at R.A.F. Waddington, Lincolnshire, England. On the night of July 3rd 1942, 420 Squadron was part of a 325 bomber raid on the German city of Bremen. Sgt Whytock was a crew member on board a Hampden I bomber, number AT248 PT-A which took off from Waddington. This bomber was shot down, having been claimed by Oblt. Egmont Prinz zur Lippe Weissenfeld of II./NJG2, and crashed at 0054hrs at Koudum, Friesland, Holland. The pilot survived and was captured while the other three members, including Sgt Whytock were killed. He was buried in Plot A, Row 1, Grave 16, Hemelumer Oldeferd (Koudum) General Cemetery, Friesland, Holland.

Service number: R56325

Medals and Awards: 1939-45 Star, Air Crew Europe Star, Defence Medal, the Canadian Volunteer Service Medal and clasp and the War Medal 1939-45.

WILSON, David
8th Bn

Private
WWI

Photo courtesy Winnipeg Tribune 1915

David Wilson was born on September 3rd 1896 in Lachute, son of David, a butcher and Agnes McFarlane. By 1911, the Wilsons were residing in Township 7, Manitoba. David enlisted with "H" Company, 8th Battalion, C.E.F. on September 21st 1914, in Valcartier, Quebec. He reported at that time that he was a tinsmith by trade. He remained in Canada until September 27th, when he boarded the troopship S.S. Franconia. The troopship left Canadian waters on October 3rd, and arrived safely in Plymouth, England on the 16th. The 8th underwent training until April 1st 1915, when the Battalion, including Pte Wilson, crossed the Channel and landed in France. The 8th Battalion proceeded to the Front and David participated in some grueling battles, including the gas attack at Ypres on April 24th 1915, in which the Battalion held its ground against a German attack. Pte Wilson remained with his unit until July 17th 1915, when he died, as a result of wounds received in action, at No.1 Canadian Field Ambulance. He was buried in Plot B, Row 2, Maple Leaf cemetery, Hainaut, Belgium.

Service number: 336

Medals and Awards: 1914-15 Star, British War Medal and Victory Medal (1914-1919).

WOLFENDALE, George H. **H/Captain**
C.C.S. **WWII**

George Hedley Wolfendale was born in Fairford, Gloucestershire, England on October 27th 1899, son of George Ashton, a physician and surgeon, and Frances Warwick. George's mother died when George was still very young and his father in 1925. He was educated in England, attending Magdalen College School, Nuneaton Grammar School and finally attending Oundle School until May 1915, when he enlisted with the Lancashire Fusiliers, to take part in World War One. After the War, he remained in England until June 16th 1921, when he arrived in Canada to settle. George attended the Montreal Diocesan Theological College from 1929 to 1931, obtaining his diocesan licence. He was now a clergyman and he left immediately for British Columbia, where he remained until 1934. George married Esther Florence Foy in Tramore, Ontario, on September 26th 1934. In 1935 he returned to Montreal for a brief period, becoming the incumbent of the parish of Arundel at the end of the year. He remained in Arundel until 1938 when he moved to the parish of Aylwin, Quebec, to become its incumbent. He remained there until 1939, when he enlisted in the Canadian Army. On November 18th 1939, George enlisted with No.9 Field Ambulance in Montreal. He remained in Canada for only a short period of time, since, on December 7th, he boarded a troopship in Halifax, Nova Scotia, and crossed the Atlantic Ocean, disembarking safely in Gourock, Scotland, on the 18th. Pte Wolfendale remained in England, training and taking courses, qualifying as a nursing orderly on June 1st 1940. On December 29th 1941, Pte Wolfendale was transferred to the Canadian Chaplain Services and promoted to the rank of Honorary Captain. H/Capt Wolfendale would find himself assigned to several units while in the United Kingdom until July 7th 1943, when he was assigned to the 1st Canadian Corps, Royal Canadian Engineers. On October 24th, he left the United Kingdom, bound for Italy and disembarked on November 8th. On May 15th 1944, H/Capt Wolfendale accompanied a reconnaissance patrol of the 12th Canadian Field Company, Royal Canadian Engineers, when he was hit by four machine pistol bullets, while in the Liri Valley, about three miles South of Cassino, Italy. He was captured by German Forces and taken to Hospital 2912, treated for severe wounds, including bullet wounds to the left elbow and knee joint, a stomach wound and inflammation of the left lung. Sadly, on June 11th 1944, H/Capt George Hedley Wolfendale died while in the German hospital. He was later buried in Plot III, Row C, Grave 5, Bologna War Cemetery, Italy. On December 29th 1944, he was appointed a Member of the Order of the British Empire (MBE). Part of the citation* for the MBE speaks to the character and dedication of this fine military Chaplain:

> *"H/Captain Wolfendale has been Chaplain with I Cdn Corps Tps Engineers since 1943 and during his period of service has become both beloved and respected by all ranks of the unit. He has devoted himself to the welfare of the men and by his efforts has maintained the moral of the unit at the highest possible level."*

* The citation card for the award is very difficult to read and only the first part was included.

Service number: D93674 - H/Captain

Medals and Awards: Member of the Most Excellent Order of the British Empire, British War Medal, Victory Medal (1914-1919), 1939-45 Star,

Italy Star, Defence Medal, the Canadian Volunteer Service Medal and clasp and the War Medal 1939-45.

Bibliography

Published sources

List of officers and men serving in the First Canadian Contingent of the British Expeditionary Force, 1914, compiled by Pay and Record Office, The Office, London, 1915

Princess Patricia's Canadian Light Infantry (reinforcements): nominal roll of officers, non-commissioned officers and men, Issued with Militia Orders 1915, Canadian Expeditionary Force, Ottawa, 1915

A short history and photographic record of the 73rd Battalion Canadian Expeditionary Force, Royal Highlanders of Canada, allied with the Black Watch, Ottawa, Mortimer, [1916?]

L. McLeod Gould, *From B.C. to Baisieux being the narrative history of the 102nd Canadian Infantry Battalion*, Thos. R. Cusack Presses, Victoria, B.C., 1919

38th Battalion also 1st and 2nd Reinforcing Drafts, nominal roll of officers, non-commissioned officers and men, Issued with Militia Orders 1915, Canadian Expeditionary Force, Ottawa, 1915

69th Battalion, nominal roll of officers, non-commissioned officers and men, Canadian Expeditionary Force, Ottawa.

52nd Battalion also 1st and 2nd Reinforcing Drafts, nominal roll of officers, non-commissioned officers and men, Issued with Militia Orders 1917, Canadian Expeditionary Force, Ottawa, 1917

53rd Battalion also 1st and 2nd Reinforcing Drafts, nominal roll of officers, non-commissioned officers and men, Issued with Militia Orders 1915, Canadian Expeditionary Force, Ottawa, 1915

24th Battalion, nominal roll of officers, non-commissioned officers and men, Issued with Militia Orders 1915, Canadian Expeditionary Force, Ottawa, 1915

2nd Infantry Brigade Headquarters and 7th Battalion, nominal roll of officers, non-commissioned officers and men, Issued with Militia Orders 1915, Canadian Expeditionary Force, Ottawa, 1915

2nd, 3rd, 4th and 5th University Companies P.P.C.L.I. Reinforcements, nominal roll of officers, non-commissioned officers and men, Issued with Militia Orders 1915, Canadian Expeditionary Force, Ottawa, 1915

1st Regiment Canadian Mounted Rifles, nominal roll of officers, non-commissioned officers and men, Issued with Militia Orders 1915, Canadian Expeditionary Force, Ottawa, 1915

41st Battalion and Reinforcing Draft, nominal roll of officers, non-commissioned officers and men, Issued with Militia Orders 1917

196th Battalion and Reinforcing Draft, nominal roll of officers, non-commissioned officers and men, Issued with Militia Orders 1917

87th Battalion, nominal roll of officers, non-commissioned officers and men, Issued with Militia Orders 1915, Canadian Expeditionary Force, Ottawa, 1915

Bird, C.W., Davies, J.B., Lieut., *The Canadian Forestry Corps, Its Inception, Development and Achievements*, H.M Stationery Office, London, 1919

Cook, Tim, *No Place to Run The Canadian Corps and Gas Warfare in the First World War*, UBC Press, Vancouver, 1999, 2009

Fetherstonhaugh, R.C., LL.D, *McGill University at War 1914-1918 1939-1945*, McGill University, Montreal, 1947

Gordon L.L. Major, *British Battles and Medals Fifth Edition*, Spink & Son Ltd, London, 1979

Thomas, C., *History of the Counties of Argenteuil, Que., & Prescott, Ont., from the earliest settlement to the present*, John Lovell & Son, Montreal, 1896

Rigby, George Reginald, *A History of Lachute, from its earliest times to January 1, 1964*, Brownsburg-Lachute Rotary Club, Brownsburg, 1964

Allison, Les and Hayward, Harry, *They Shall Grow Not Old*, Commonwealth Air Training Plan Museum Inc., Brandon, 1995

Nicholson, G.W.L., Lt.-Col., *Official History of the Canadian Army in the First World War, Canadian Expeditionary Force 1914-1919,* Queen's Printers, Ottawa 1964

Nicholson, G.W.L., Lt.-Col., *Official History of the Canadian Army in the Second World War, Volume II, The Canadians in Italy*, Queen's Printers, Ottawa 1956

Wigney Edward H., *Serial Numbers of the C.E.F.*, E.H. Wigney, Nepean, 1996

Law, Clive M., *Regimental Numbers of the Canadian Army 1936-1960 Revised second edition*, Service Publications, Ottawa, 2008

Colledge, J.J. and Warlow, Ben, *Ships of the Royal Navy The Complete Record of all Fighting Ships of the Royal Navy from the 15th Century to the Present,* Fully Revised and Updated, Casemate, Newbury, 2010

Henshaw, Trevor, *The Sky Their Battlefield*, Grub Street, London, 1995

Chorley W.R., *Royal Air Force Bomber Command Losses of the Second World War*, 9 volumes, Midland Publishing, Hinckley, 2004

Middlebrook, Martin/ Everitt, Chris, *The Bomber Command War Diaries An operational reference book: 1939-1945*, Penguin Group, London, 1985

Jordan, Roger, *The World's Merchant Fleets 1939, The Particulars and Wartime fates of 6,000 ships*, Naval Institute Press, Annapolis, 2006

Montreal From 1535 to 1914, Biographical, Volume III, The S.J. Clarke Publishing Company, Montreal, 1914

Erskine, Douglas, *A Bit of Atlantis*, A.T. Chapman, Montreal, 1900

The Ottawa City Directory 1916, Volume XLIII, Might Directories Limited, Ottawa, 1916

Alderson, Robert, *Milles Isles Presbyterian Cemetery Argenteuil County*, Quebec Family History Society, Pointe Claire, 1989

LeRossignol, Suzanne/Redmile, Pennie, St.Andrew's East Protestant Cemetery, Quebec Family History Society, Pointe Claire, 1990-1991

McGill Honour Roll 1914-1918, McGill University, Montreal, 1926

Harvest Leave for members of C.E.F., (The Montreal Gazette), Montreal, Quebec, 10th of August 1918, page 10, column 2

Morgan, Henry James, *Canadian men and women of the time, Second Edition*, William Briggs, Toronto, 1912

Scott, A.G.L., *Sixty Squadron R.A.F. A History of the squadron from its formation*, William Heinemann, London, 1920

Duguid, A. Fortescue, *Official History of the Canadian Force in the Great War 1914-1919*, 2 volumes, Minister of National Defence, Ottawa, 1938

Canada. Department of Militia and Defence. The Militia List. Ottawa: Queen's Printer, 1863–1929. Library and Archives Canada, Ottawa, Ontario, Canada.

Samuel Pedlar, *Ancestral History of Charles Pedlar of Vauxhall, Cornwall, England, born about 1710, And His Descendants, also Edward Morrish of St. Stephens, Cornwall, England, born about 1765 And His Descendants*, Hunter Rose & Co., Toronto, 1894.

Bishop's 34 The Year Book of the University of Bishop's College, 1934

Bishop's 35 The Year Book of the University of Bishop's College, 1935

West Hill High School, *Annual*, Montreal, 1944

Jefford, C.G. MBE, BA, RAF (Retd), *R.A.F. Squadrons, A comprehensive record of the movement and equipment of all RAF Squadrons and their antecedents since 1912*, Airlife Publishing Limited, Shrewsbury, 2001

Franks, Norman L.R., *Royal Air Force Fighter Command Losses of the Second World War, Volume 1 Operational Losses: Airraft and Crews 1939-1941*, Revised Edition, Midland Publishing Limited, Hersham, 2008.

Greenhous, Brereton, Harris, Stephen J., Johnston, William C., Rawling, William G.P., *The Crucible of War 1939-1945 The Official History of the Royal Canadian Air Force*, Volume III, University of Toronto Press Inc., Department of National Defence and Canadian Government Publishing Centre, Supply and Services Canada, Canada 1994.

The Evening Citizen, Ottawa, Ontario, 1945.

Thomas David A., *Crete 1941 the battle at sea*, Efstathiadis Group, Athens, 1991.

Archival Records

Library and Archives Canada (L.A.C.), RG9 Militia and Defence, Series III-D-3, War Diaries of the First World War

Library and Archives Canada (L.A.C.), RG24 National Defence, Second World War Service Files: Canadian Armed Forces War Dead
Library and Archives Canada (L.A.C.), RG24 National Defence, Series C-3, War Diaries, 1939-1967

Library and Archives Canada (L.A.C.), RG24 National Defence, Series E-7, R.C.A.F. Operational Record Books, 1936-1965

Library and Archives Canada (L.A.C.), RG31, Statistics Canada, Census of Canada, 1891

Library and Archives Canada (L.A.C.), RG31, Statistics Canada, Census of Canada, 1901

Library and Archives Canada (L.A.C.), RG31, Statistics Canada, Census of Canada, 1911

Library and Archives Canada (L.A.C.), RG31, Statistics Canada, Census of Canada, 1916

Library and Archives Canada (L.A.C.), RG 76-C. Department of Employment and Immigration Fonds, Passenger Lists, 1865–1935

Library and Archives Canada (L.A.C.), RG150 Ministry of the Overseas Military Forces of Canada, Soldiers of the First World War – CEF

Library and Archives Canada (L.A.C.), RG 150 Ministry of the Overseas Military Forces of Canada, 1992–1993/314, Boxes 145–238 War Graves Registry: Circumstances of Death Records

Library and Archives Canada (L.A.C.) – Microform Digitization - Veterans Death Cards: First World War

Library and Archives Canada (L.A.C.) – A Nation's Chronicle: The Canada Gazette

Library and Archives Canada (L.A.C.) - RG 76-C. Department of Employment and Immigration fonds, Passenger Lists, 1865–1935, Microfilm Publications T-479 to T-520, T-4689 to T-4874, T-14700 to T-14939, C-4511 to C-4542

United States National Archives (N.A.R.A.), National Personnel Records Centre (N.P.R.C.), St-Louis, Missouri, U.S.A.

The National Archives (T.N.A.), Kew, Richmond, Surrey, United Kingdom, Records of the Admiralty, Naval Forces, Royal Marines, Coastguard, and related bodies, ADM188, Royal Navy Registers of Seamen's Services, 1853-1924

The National Archives (T.N.A.), Kew, Richmond, Surrey, United Kingdom, Air Ministry: Records of the Royal Air Force, AIR 27, Operations Record Books, Squadrons

The National Archives (T.N.A.), Kew, Richmond, Surrey, United Kingdom, Air Ministry: Records of the Royal Air Force, AIR 1, Operations Record Books, Squadrons

The National Archives (T.N.A.), Kew, Richmond, Surrey, United Kingdom, Air Ministry: Department of the Master-General of Personnel, AIR 76, Officers' Service Records

The National Archives (T.N.A.), Kew, Richmond, Surrey, United Kingdom, War Office: Records created or inherited by the War Office, Armed Forces, Judge Advocate General, and related bodies, WO 126, Local Armed Forces, Enrolment Forms, South African War.

The National Archives (T.N.A.), Kew, Richmond, Surrey, United Kingdom, War Office: Records created or inherited by the War Office, Armed Forces, Judge Advocate General, and related bodies, Records of the Commander-in-Chief, Military Secretary and Army Council, WO 373, War Office and Ministry of Defence: Military Secretary's Department: Recommendations for Honours and Awards for Gallant and

Distinguished Service (Army), COMBATANT GALLANTRY AWARDS, North West Europe, 21 Dec 1944 (part)-1 Feb 1945.

The National Archives (T.N.A.), Kew, Richmond, Surrey, United Kingdom, War Office: Campaign Medal and Award Rolls 1793-1949 (General Series). The National Archives microfilm publication WO 100, 241 rolls.

The National Archives (T.N.A.), Kew, Richmond, Surrey, United Kingdom, Records of the Board of Trade and of successor and related bodies, BT 389, Registry of shipping and seamen: War of 1939-1945; Merchant shipping movement cards.

Royal Air Force Museum (R.A.F.M.), Grahame Park Way, London, United Kingdom, Casualty cards.

The National Museum of the Royal Navy, HM Naval Base (PP66), Portsmouth, PO1 3NH, United Kingdom, Casualties in Action 1939-1945.

National Archives of South Africa (N.A.S.A.), Western Cape Provincial Archives and Records Service, Cape Town Archives Repository, Defence Documents, Cape Mounted Rifles Defaulters, 72 Roeland Street, CAPE TOWN, South Africa

Scotiabank Group Archives, the Bank of Ottawa Guarantee Fund, Active & Enlisted Staff (Staff Lists), 1907-1918, 44 King Street West, 19th Floor, Toronto, ON, M5H 1H1

Home Office, Identity and Passport Services, General Register Office (G.R.O.), Certificates of Births, PO Box 2, Southport, Merseyside, PR8 2JD, United Kingdom

Online databases

BMS2000, Recherche Généalogique en ligne, < http://www.bms2000.org>, 2013

Généalogie Quebec, http://www.genealogiequebec.com/default.aspx 2013, Institut généalogique Drouin 490 Charles-Péguy Est, La Prairie, Quebec, Mariages et décès 1926-1996.

Généalogie Quebec, http://www.genealogiequebec.com/default.aspx 2013, Institut généalogique Drouin 490 Charles-Péguy Est, La Prairie, Quebec, Nécrologe.

Commonwealth War Graves Commission (C.W.G.C.), casualty database, <http://www.cwgc.org/> 2012, 2 Marlow Road Maidenhead Berkshire, United Kingdom.

Veterans Affairs Canada, Canadian Virtual War Memorial online database <http://www.veterans.gc.ca>

ScotlandsPeople, Statutory Births 1855-2011, <http://www.scotlandspeople.gov.uk/search/birth/index.aspx>, National Records of Scotland and the Court of the Lord Lyon, Scotland, 2012

ScotlandsPeople, Statutory Marriages 1855-2011, <http://www.scotlandspeople.gov.uk/search/birth/index.aspx>, National Records of Scotland and the Court of the Lord Lyon, Scotland, 2012

Ancestry.com. *Quebec, Vital and Church Records (Drouin Collection), 1621-1967* [database on-line]. Provo, UT, USA: Ancestry.com Operations Inc, 2008. Original data: Gabriel Drouin, comp. *Drouin Collection*. Montreal, Quebec, Canada: Institut Généalogique Drouin.

Ancestry.com. *Ontario, Canada, Catholic Church Records (Drouin Collection), 1747-1967* [database on-line]. Provo, UT, USA: Ancestry.com Operations Inc, 2007. Original data: Gabriel Drouin, comp. *Drouin Collection*. Montreal, Quebec, Canada: Institut Généalogique Drouin.

Ancestry.com. *Ontario, Canada Births, 1869-1913* [database on-line]. Provo, UT, USA: Ancestry.com Operations Inc, 2010. Original data: Archives of Ontario.

Ancestry.com and Genealogical Research Library (Brampton, Ontario, Canada). *Ontario, Canada, Marriages, 1801-1928* [database on-line]. Provo, UT, USA: Ancestry.com Operations, Inc., 2010. Original data: Ontario, Canada. *Registrations of Marriages, 1869-1928*. MS932, Reels 1-833, 850-880. Archives of Ontario, Toronto.

Ancestry.com. *Canadian Passenger Lists, 1865-1935* [database on-line]. Provo, UT, USA: Ancestry.com Operations Inc, 2010. Original data: *Passenger Lists, 1865–1935*. Microfilm Publications T-479 to T-520, T-4689 to T-4874, T-14700 to T-14939, C-4511 to C-4542. Library and Archives Canada, n.d. RG 76-C. Department of Employment and Immigration fonds. Library and Archives Canada Ottawa, Ontario, Canada.

Ancestry.com. *Canada, Ocean Arrivals (Form 30A), 1919-1924* [database on-line]. Provo, UT, USA: Ancestry.com Operations, Inc., 2009. Original data: Library and Archives Canada. *Form 30A, 1919-1924 (Ocean Arrivals)*. Ottawa, Ontario, Canada: Library and Archives Canada, n.d. RG 76. Department of Employment and Immigration Fonts. Microfilm Reels: T-14939 to T-15248.

Ancestry.com. *Border Crossings: From Canada to U.S., 1895-1954* [database on-line]. Provo, UT, USA: Ancestry.com Operations, Inc., 2010. Original data: *Records of the Immigration and Naturalization Service, RG 85*. Washington, D.C.: National Archives and Records Administration.

Ancestry.com. *British Columbia, Canada, Marriage Index, 1872-1935* [database on-line]. Provo, UT, USA: Ancestry.com Operations Inc, 2001. Original data: British Columbia Vital Statistics Agency. British Columbia, Canada. British Columbia Vital Statistics Agency: P.O. Box 9657, Stn Prov Govt, Victoria, BC V8W 9P3.

Ancestry.com. 1901 England Census [database on-line]. Provo, UT, USA: Ancestry.com Operations Inc, 2005. Original data: Census Returns of England and Wales, 1901. Kew, Surrey, England: The National Archives, 1901. Data imaged from the National Archives, London, England.

Ancestry.com. 1911 England Census [database on-line]. Provo, UT, USA: Ancestry.com Operations, Inc., 2011. Original data: Census Returns of England and Wales, 1911. Kew, Surrey, England: The National Archives of the UK (TNA), 1911. Data imaged from the National Archives, London, England.

Ancestry.com. British Army WWI Medal Rolls Index Cards, 1914-1920 [database on-line]. Provo, UT, USA: Ancestry.com Operations Inc, 2008. Original data: Army Medal Office. WWI Medal Index Cards. In the care of The Western Front Association website.

Ancestry.com. *London, England, Births and Baptisms, 1813-1906* [database on-line]. Provo, UT, USA: Ancestry.com Operations, Inc., 2010.

Original data: Board of Guardian Records, 1834-1906 and Church of England Parish Registers, 1754-1906. London Metropolitan Archives, London.

Ancestry.com. *British Army WWI Service Records, 1914-1920* [database on-line]. Provo, UT, USA: Ancestry.com Operations Inc, 2008. Original data: The National Archives of the UK (TNA): Public Record Office (PRO). War Office: Soldiers' Documents, First World War 'Burnt Documents' (Microfilm Copies); (The National Archives Microfilm Publication WO363); Records created or inherited by the War Office, Armed Forces, Judge Advocate General, and related bodies; The National Archives of the UK (TNA), Kew, Surrey, England.

Ancestry.com. *UK, Outward Passenger Lists, 1890-1960* [database on-line]. Provo, UT, USA: Ancestry.com Operations, Inc., 2012. Original data: Board of Trade: Commercial and Statistical Department and successors: Outwards Passenger Lists. BT27. Records of the Commercial, Companies, Labour, Railways and Statistics Departments. Records of the Board of Trade and of successor and related bodies. The National Archives, Kew, Richmond, Surrey, England.

Ancestry.com. *UK, Incoming Passenger Lists, 1878-1960* [database on-line]. Provo, UT, USA: Ancestry.com Operations Inc, 2008. Original data: *Board of Trade: Commercial and Statistical Department and successors: Inwards Passenger Lists*. Kew, Surrey, England: The National Archives of the UK (TNA). Series BT26, 1,472 pieces.

Ancestry.com. England & Wales, National Probate Calendar (Index of Wills and Administrations), 1858-1966 [database on-line]. Provo, UT, USA:

Ancestry.com Operations Inc, 2010. Original data: Principal Probate Registry. Calendar of the Grants of Probate and Letters of Administration made in the Probate Registries of the High Court of Justice in England. London, England © Crown copyright.

Ancestry.com. Canada, Nominal Rolls and Paylists for the Volunteer Militia, 1857-1922 [database on-line]. Provo, UT, USA: Ancestry.com Operations, Inc., 2010. This collection was indexed by Ancestry World Archives Project contributors. Original data: Department of Militia and Defence, Accounts and Pay Branch, Nominal Rolls and Paylists for the Volunteer Militia, 1885-1914. R180-100-9-E, formerly RG9-II-F-6, 138 rolls. Library and Archives Canada, Ottawa, Ontario.

Ancestry.com. *Canada, Voters Lists, 1935-1980* [database on-line]. Provo, UT, USA: Ancestry.com Operations, Inc., 2012. Original data: Voters Lists, Federal Elections, 1935–1980. R1003-6-3-E (RG113-B). Library and Archives Canada, Ottawa, Ontario, Canada.

Ancestry.com. Canada, Military Honours and Awards Citation Cards, 1900-1961 [database on-line]. Provo, UT, USA: Ancestry.com Operations, Inc., 2012. Original data: Honours and Awards Citation Cards. Ottawa, Ontario, Canada: Library and Archives Canada.

The London Gazette PO Box 7923 London, England, online archives database < http://www.london-gazette.co.uk>

Dictionary of Canadian Biography Online, database < http://www.biographi.ca/index-e.html> 2011

New Brunswick, Provincial Returns of Births and Late Registrations, 1810-1906," index and images, *FamilySearch* <https://familysearch.org>

Royal BC Museum, <http://royalbcmuseum.bc.ca/MainSite/ >, BC Archives Genealogy, births (1854-1903), marriages (1872-1936), deaths (1872-1991), colonial marriages (1859-1872) and baptisms (1836-1888), 2012

Bibliothèque et Archives nationales du Quebec,< http://www.banq.qc.ca> Collections numériques, Annuaires Lovell de Montreal et sa banlieue (1842-1999), 2012

"Ireland Births and Baptisms, 1620-1881," index, *FamilySearch, <* http://www.familysearch.org *>, 2013*

Uboat.net, <http://uboat.net/index.html>, 2013

31290514R00125

Made in the USA
Charleston, SC
13 July 2014